BARACK OBAMA

"We Are One People"

Revised and Expanded

Michael A. Schuman

Series Consultant:
Dr. Russell L. Adams, Chairman
Department of
Afro-American Studies,
Howard University

Enslow Publishers, Inc.
40 Industrial Road
Box 398
Berkeley Heights, NJ 07922
USA

http://www.enslow.com

"WE ARE ONE PEOPLE, ALL OF US PLEDGING
ALLEGIANCE TO THE STARS AND STRIPES, ALL OF US
DEFENDING THE UNITED STATES OF AMERICA."
—*Barack Obama*

Library of Congress Cataloging-in-Publication Data

Schuman, Michael.
    Barack Obama : "we are one people" / Michael A. Schuman. — Rev. and expanded
      p. cm. — (African-American biography library)
    Includes bibliographical references and index.
    Summary: "A biography of Barack Obama, the 44th president of the United States and
the first African American to hold the office"—Provided by publisher.
    ISBN-13: 978-0-7660-3649-9
    ISBN-10: 0-7660-3649-9
    1. Obama, Barack—Juvenile literature. 2. Legislators—United States—Biography—
Juvenile literature. 3. African American legislators—Biography—Juvenile literature.
4. United States. Congress. Senate—Biography—Juvenile literature. 5. Racially mixed
people—United States—Biography—Juvenile literature. I. Title.
    E901.1.O23S23 2009
    973.932092—dc22
    [B]   2008053678

Contents

Barack Obama delivers his keynote address to delegates
during the Democratic National Convention in Boston, July 27, 2004,
during his run for United States senator of Illinois.

◆◆◆◆◆

Chapter 1

On Stage in Front of the World

I t was an unlikely place to be for a man who refers to himself as a "skinny guy from the Southside [of Chicago] with a funny name."[1] The Southside is one of Chicago's poorest and toughest neighborhoods. The man's name is often misunderstood when people first hear it.

Whenever he spoke to a new group, this man lightened the mood by cracking a joke about his name. He would say something like, "People would ask me where did you get this funny name, Barack Obama, although they wouldn't say it right. They would call me 'Alabama' or they would call me 'Yo Mama.' I'd have to explain to them, 'No, it's O-bama.' My father was from Kenya, from

Africa, which is where I got my name from. My mother was from Kansas, which is where I got my accent from."[2]

Barack Obama was a state senator from Illinois, running for a seat in the United States Senate. Yet, there he was on stage in front of the world.

The date was Tuesday, July 27, 2004. The setting was the Democratic National Convention in Boston, Massachusetts. Obama was about to deliver the keynote address, one of the most important speeches at any political convention. The purpose of a keynote address is to set the tone for the entire event.

PROFILE

Obama gets keynote spot

The Democrats tapped Barack Obama, an Illinois state senator running for the U.S. Senate, to be the keynote speaker at their convention.

Name — Barack Obama
Age/birth date — 42, Aug. 4, 1961
Education — Law degree, Harvard University; political science degree, Columbia University
Experience — State senator; law professor, University of Chicago
Family — Wife, Michelle; two daughters

AP

The person assigned to give a keynote address is usually well known, such as a sitting governor or senator. So why would Barack Obama, who was relatively unknown outside of Illinois, be given such an important assignment?

One reason was his charisma. Obama is an exciting speaker. In addition, the vast majority of keynote speakers have been white males. Yet even among African-American political candidates, Obama was different. Most have roots in the American civil rights movement of the 1950s and 1960s.

Obama is too young to have had an active role in the civil rights movement. He was only six when Martin Luther King, Jr., was assassinated. Obama represents Americans of a new era. He was born in 1961. Because of his unusual background, he appeals to both African Americans and whites.

Yet on that day in the summer of 2004 there was one huge, outstanding question. Could this little-known politician handle a keynote address that would be televised across the world? When a reporter asked him that morning if he was nervous, Obama honestly answered yes. Yet he admitted there are people with much bigger problems than his. He replied, "There's going to be some adrenaline. But the pressure I'm experiencing is nothing compared to folks I'm meeting getting laid off . . . That's real pressure."[3]

In his Chicago Senate-campaign office on July 22, 2004,
Barack Obama reads through the twenty-minute keynote address he
would deliver to the Democratic National Convention.

After he took the podium that night, Obama first spoke about his unusual family. He then discussed the greatness of the United States, and quoted from the Declaration of Independence. He praised the Democratic presidential nominee, Massachusetts Senator John Kerry. But what seemed to most capture the hearts of his audience was his discussion of unity in America. The United States had been portrayed in recent months by both journalists and private citizens as a divided country.

Obama said:

> Now even as we speak, there are those who are preparing to divide us, the spin masters and negative ad peddlers who embrace the politics of anything goes.
>
> Well, I say to them tonight, there's not a liberal America and a conservative America—there is the United States of America.
>
> There's not a black America and white America and Latino America and Asian America—there is the United States of America.

Television newscasters use a United States map as a visual aid when showing the progress of presidential elections. The states won by the Democratic candidate are colored blue. Those won by the Republican candidate are colored red. Obama referred to this as he continued.

> The pundits like to slice and dice our country into red states and blue states; red states for Republicans, blue states for Democrats. But I've got news for them, too. We worship an awesome God in the blue

Barack Obama and his wife, Michelle, wave to the crowd
after he delivered his keynote address to the Democratic National
Convention in Boston on July 27, 2004.

states, and we don't like federal agents poking around our libraries in the red states.

We coach Little League in the blue states and have gay friends in the red states.

There are patriots who opposed the war in Iraq and patriots who supported it.

We are one people, all of us pledging allegiance to the stars and stripes, all of us defending the United States of America.[4]

The speech was a smash. In less than an hour, Barack Obama became a household name. Journalist Tina Brown wrote, "Two days later when Obama emerged from the convention hall in Boston to climb into a modest white sedan he was mobbed like P. Diddy."[5]

Political analyst Carlos Watson wrote simply, "He's got the potential not just to be a star, but to be a super-star."[6]

A political satirist named Mo Rocca was asked to grade Obama's speech, A through F. Rocca gave Obama a special grade—an O+. Rocca wrote, "He gets an O for Obamatastic. Overall, he gets an O+ because the pressure was so high. Anyone would have choked—except Obama."[7]

Barack Obama was born in Honolulu, Hawaii.

Chapter 2

Life With Tutu and Lolo

Barack Hussein Obama may have represented Illinois as a United States senator, but he was born in a more exotic place: Honolulu, Hawaii. In fact, when Obama was born on August 4, 1961, Hawaii had been a state for less than two years. Most Hawaiians then were either of Asian descent or white Americans working on a military base.

Obama's parents were very different from the majority of Hawaiians. His mother, Ann, was a white woman who had grown up in small towns in Texas, Oklahoma, and Kansas. His father, Barack Hussein Obama, Sr., was an African Muslim born in a small village in Kenya called Alego. Both Ann and Barack, Sr., were students at the University of Hawaii. Barack, Sr., was the first African student in the university's history.

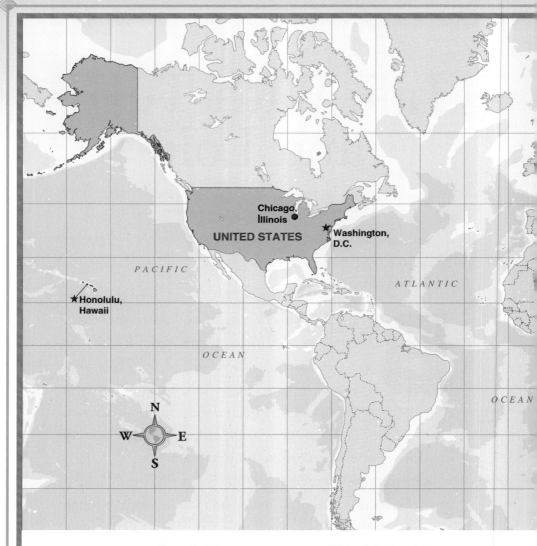

Chicago, Illinois

UNITED STATES

Washington, D.C.

PACIFIC

ATLANTIC

Honolulu, Hawaii

OCEAN

OCEAN

N
W
E
S

Barack Obama spent most of his childhood in
Honolulu, Hawaii, except for the years that he lived in a village
outside of Jakarta, Indonesia.

His father returned to Kenya when Barack was very young.
As an adult, Barack would make Chicago his home and eventually
serve as a United States senator in Washington, D.C.

The two began dating in 1960, which was a brave thing to do. In much of the United States at the time, it was risky for black and white people to date. That was especially true in the South where legal segregation, or separation of the races, was the law. Obama said, "In many parts of the South, my father could have been strung up from a tree for merely looking at my mother the wrong way."[1]

Despite their backgrounds Ann and Barack, Sr., found they had much in common. They shared the same views about religion. Although Barack, Sr.'s parents were Muslims, he had become an atheist. To Barack, Sr., religion was little more than superstition.[2] Interestingly, the name "Barack" means "blessing from God." Ann had grown up in a family with a Christian background, but found her fellow Christians tended to be narrow-minded.[3] Yet she enjoyed studying different religions, and found valuable ideas in each.

Shortly after Barack, Sr., and Ann began dating they were married. Interracial marriage was illegal in much of the United States. However, Hawaii was a new state and did not share the legal history or social traditions of the rest of the nation. Barack, Sr., and Ann were not bothered much by others about their marriage.

Barack, Jr., was born while his father was a student. Barack, Sr., graduated the next year, 1962, with a bachelor's degree in economics. Instead of getting a job right away,

A Racist Episode

Ann and Barack, Sr., were not confronted too often over their interracial marriage. However there was some racism in Hawaii. One time after an evening of studying, Barack, Sr., went to a local bar to relax with some friends. Ann's father, who Barack, Jr., called Gramps, joined them, too. Gramps said that while they were at the bar, a white man loudly referred to Barack's father by a derogatory name for African Americans. Barack, Sr., stood up and walked over to the man. The onlookers expected the two to break into a no-holds-barred bar fight.

Instead, Barack, Sr., talked to the man who insulted him. He told him how hurtful bigotry is. He also said that all people have the same human rights. Barack, Sr.'s message sunk in. The man who had insulted Barack's father felt so bad that he apologized by giving him one hundred dollars.

Barack, Sr., decided he wanted to get a master's degree, or advanced college degree. Having a master's degree in addition to his bachelor's degree might help him get an even better job in economics.

Barack, Sr., was offered a very generous scholarship at a highly regarded university called The New School in New York City. If he had taken the scholarship, he would have been able to afford to bring his young family with him while he continued his studies.

At the same time, he was also offered a smaller scholarship at Harvard University in Cambridge, Massachusetts. Harvard is one of the most highly regarded universities in the world. Barack, Sr., felt he could not afford to turn down the chance to earn an advanced degree from Harvard.

> Barack, Sr., . . . moved to Massachusetts by himself, leaving his wife and infant son in Hawaii.

There was one big problem. The Harvard scholarship would pay for his studies, but did not include enough money for him to support his family.

Barack, Sr., made a tough decision. He moved to Massachusetts by himself, leaving his wife and infant son in Hawaii. When he could afford it, or when he had completed his Harvard studies, the family would reunite. Perhaps they would move to Kenya where Barack, Sr., would have his choice of rewarding jobs as an economist.

However, something unexpected happened. The longer Barack, Sr., and Ann were away from each other, the more they lost interest in their marriage. Eventually Barack, Sr., returned to Kenya by himself. He embarked on a career as an economist, and got an important job in the Kenyan government. He also remarried and raised a new family.

Barack, Jr., continued to live with his mother, but also spent much time with his grandparents. Although his grandmother was a white woman from the mainland United States, she was given a Hawaiian nickname, Tutu. It means "grandparent" in Hawaiian. Barack called her "Toot" for short. Meanwhile, Barack was given a nickname that made him sound less foreign: Barry.

It was not long before Barry's mother began to see another man. Like Barry's father, this man was a student from another country at the University of Hawaii. His name was Lolo Soetoro, and he was from Indonesia. By coincidence, Lolo means "crazy" in Hawaiian, but this man was very mild mannered. When he was not with Ann, he spent time playing chess with Gramps or playfully wrestling with Barry. After about two years, Lolo and Ann were married.

The marriage meant a huge change in Barry's life. In 1967, his mother and stepfather made plans to move to Indonesia. Lolo left for home right away. At first, Ann and Barry stayed behind. They had to apply for

Barack Obama visits the Masai Mara game reserve in
Kenya on August 30, 2006. Barack Obama's father moved back to
Kenya when Barack was very young.

◆◆◆◆◆

documents such as passports and visas that are necessary for Americans who travel to certain countries. Since there were illnesses in Indonesia not found in the United States, Ann and Barry had to be given many immunizations before they moved to their new home.

After a few months, the mother and son flew to Indonesia's capital, Jakarta. Lolo drove them to his home, a humble stucco and red tile structure with a big mango tree in the front yard. Barry was shocked to see a pet that Lolo had bought for him: an ape named Tata. He was stunned to see even more animals in his new backyard, including chickens, ducks, a dog, a cockatoo, and two baby crocodiles.

> He saw unimaginable poverty on the streets of Jakarta.

Barry could see that life in Indonesia was going to be very different from what it had been in Hawaii. He saw unimaginable poverty on the streets of Jakarta. Beggars seemed to be everywhere. They had nothing in their possession but the worn and torn clothing they wore. Many had suffered strange diseases and had mangled bodies. There were beggars without arms, and some without feet who walked on their hands. Others without legs moved around on makeshift carts.

Still more were victims of polio and leprosy, diseases that had long since disappeared from the United States. Some wandered the streets asking for handouts, while others came to people's houses, knocking on doors and begging for money.

At first, Ann willingly gave money to these unfortunate people. It was simply her nature to do so.

An Indonesian journalist who knew Ann wrote, "Ann was one of the kindest, most warm-hearted, sensitive, generous people I have known . . . When I remember her, it's always her smile that appears in my mind."[4]

But Lolo put a stop to that practice. It was not that Lolo did not care about these unfortunate people. But as a native of Indonesia, he was used to living in a place with countless poor. He saw his wife and son giving a lot of their money away. He knew they could not afford to help every beggar who came to their door. Lolo told Barry it was better to save his money and make sure he did not end up living on the street some day.

Barry also got used to eating a varied diet with strange foods. One of the staples of Indonesia is rice. But Barry also sampled such tasty meals as dog meat, snake meat, and grasshoppers. He said the dog and snake meat were tough while the grasshoppers were crunchy.

Barry also discovered that despite the shots he had been given, he was very susceptible to diseases common in Indonesia. Within a few months he had both measles and chicken pox.

Most American children in Jakarta went to a private school called the International School. These students

In this undated photograph, Obama is shown circled in a group photo during a graduation ceremony at the SDN Menteng 1 school in Jakarta, Indonesia.

were mainly the sons and daughters of American diplomats and businessmen. However, Lolo and Ann did not have the money to enroll Barry in the International School. Instead, he attended local public schools where hitting students was a regular form of punishment. It was here that Barry experienced the pain of a bamboo switch.

Ann supplemented Barry's education with lessons from an American correspondence course. In a correspondence course, the student receives lessons and tests through the mail. Every weekday, Ann would awaken Barry at about 4 o'clock in the morning to go over material she received from the correspondence course. Then Barry would attend his regular public school for a normal day of lessons. Neither mother nor son was thrilled with the long hours. Barry often tried lame excuses to get out of the early-morning lessons. It did not matter. Ann thought this American-based material was too important to omit.

On some occasions, Barry received lessons on his own that were not scheduled. One day when he was nine, Barry was killing time in a library at the American embassy in Jakarta while his mother was working. He came across a collection of *Life* magazines and began browsing through them.

As he flipped through one magazine, his eyes froze on a photograph of a man whose skin seemed to have been bleached. At first, Barry thought the man must have been the victim of a strange accident or illness. As he read the text with the photo, Barry realized the man was an African American who paid to be given a chemical treatment to try and make himself look whiter.

The article said that the man later regretted going through the chemical treatment. Yet Barry wondered how many other African-American men and women

> Barry often tried lame excuses to get out of the early-morning lessons.

were so unhappy in their skin that they tried to do the same thing. Mostly though, Barry felt anger.[5]

He wrote, "When I got home that night from the embassy library, I went into the bathroom and stood in front of the mirror with all my senses and limbs seemingly intact, looking as I had always looked, and wondered if something was wrong with me."[6]

Chapter 3

Days at Punahou

By 1971, Ann had finished teaching Barry the material from the correspondence course. She felt that for her son to get the best education possible, he needed to attend an American school. That meant moving back to Hawaii.

Meanwhile, another member was added to the family. Ann and Lolo had a child, a girl they named Maya. However, neither Ann, Lolo, nor Maya would be traveling to Hawaii with Barry. He was moving there alone.

Barry's mother told him she and the rest of the family would join him in Hawaii later. In the meantime, he would live with Gramps and Toot. When he landed in Honolulu, his grandparents met him at the airport. They drove Barry to his new home: a two-bedroom apartment in a high-rise building in the city.

Barry learned from his grandfather that he would not attend a public school. Gramps's boss was a graduate of one of Hawaii's best preparatory, or prep, schools. Prep schools are private, not public, which means they are not supported by a community's taxes. Instead, students are responsible for paying for their own education. Some people believe prep school graduates have a better chance of being accepted by the college of their choice.

Not anyone can attend a prep school. Students have to be accepted based on factors such as their grades and extracurricular activities. Sometimes knowing a person connected to a prep school can help. Barry admits he was seriously considered mainly through the help of his grandfather's boss.[1]

The prep school Barry attended was Punahou School. It consisted of several buildings, including tennis courts, swimming pools, and photography studios. Nowadays some public schools have such features. However, they were rare in 1971.

> Barry had to adjust to being the new kid in class.

At ten years old, Barry had to adjust to being the new kid in class. Most of his classmates had been together since kindergarten. His teacher was a middle-aged woman named Miss Hefty. When she read Barry's full name out loud on the first day, the other children laughed at its foreign, funny sound.

Hefty had once taught school in Kenya, so she took a special interest in Barry. When she asked what tribe his father was from, the children laughed again. After Barry answered that his father was from the Luo tribe, one boy repeated the word "Luo," making it sound like a monkey's grunt. Later during Barry's first day, a girl asked if she could touch his hair. When he refused, she acted hurt. Another boy asked him if his father ate people.

On a day not long afterwards, a tall, redheaded girl decided it would be fun to pick on him because of his hair style. She was unfamiliar with the natural hair of people of African descent. One of Obama's classmates, Bernice Bowers, remembered:

> We were all on a staircase about 7:45 that morning waiting to enter Castle Hall where fifth and sixth graders had class for the day. She was teasing him like she would tease a girl for wearing a purple skirt. She teased him like his hair style was a choice he had made in dressing that day.
>
> He told her to stop it. Then she reached over and tried to touch his hair. He almost tripped trying to back away. I think she tried touching it three or four times and he was stumbling trying to get away. I was a very, mousy quiet girl watching from the side. We had all been sitting and watching and not intervening, but after it was clear his feelings had been hurt we tried to jump in and told her to stop it.[2]

Barack "Barry" Obama (third row second from left) is seen in this 1976 class photo from the Punahou School yearbook.

Bowers said there were a lot of social cliques at Punahou. She explained:

> Punahou students were very conscious of what kids wore, what kind of car your family drove—noticing what kind of car dropped you off at school—and how much money your family made. When Barry first came to Punahou from Indonesia he wore sandals over white socks. It was the first year that shoes were required at Punahou—through fourth grade you

could go to school barefoot. He got teased for that, and I think that he took it to heart. Everyone got teased at some point and it could be brutal at times. It was sort of an art form, beginning in middle school at Punahou. But he took it to heart.[3]

After awhile, the other kids got used to Barry, although he continued to feel different from his classmates.[4] He was one of the few African-American children in the entire school. He did not play the same sports they did. He grew up in Indonesia playing soccer and badminton. The kids in Hawaii played baseball and football, and liked to ride their skateboards. Barry knew nothing about those sports. When he tried, he was not very good at them.

As promised, Barry's mother returned to Hawaii that fall with Maya. However, their visit would last just a few months. She planned to return to Indonesia to join Lolo after New Year's Day.

Barry would also be joined by an unexpected visitor. His real father was coming for a visit. Barry had not seen Barack, Sr., since he was two. His mother had kept in touch with Barack, Sr., when she was in Indonesia. She told Barry about Barack, Sr.'s second family. Barry learned that he had five half brothers and one half sister in Kenya. She also told Barry that his father had been in a serious car accident at home. The trip to Hawaii was part of his long recovery process.

When Barack, Sr., arrived, he gave Barry some gifts from Africa. These included figurines of a lion, an elephant, and a man playing a drum. But Barry had not seen his father in eight long years and felt awkward around him.[5] He noticed right away that his father did not resemble the strong figure of his faint memories.

The car accident had taken a toll on Barack, Sr. He was thin and bony, and walked with a limp. When his father took off his glasses, Barry noticed his eyes had a yellowish tint. That was a sign that his father contracted malaria after he had returned to Kenya.

Barry Obama, at right, smiles in this 1979 senior yearbook photo of the Ka Wai Ola Club at Punahou School.

At school, Barry learned that Miss Hefty invited Barack, Sr., to speak to his class. Barack, Sr., told the class about animals that ran wild in his homeland that Americans could see only in zoos. He talked about tribal customs, like the rite of passage among some tribes that required a boy to kill a lion before becoming a man. He also told how the British colonized Kenya just as they did the United States two hundred years earlier. He said that Kenyans wanted to be free to govern themselves just as Americans did.

When Barack, Sr., was finished, the class burst into a huge round of applause and asked questions. The boy who had once asked Barry if his father ate people went up to Barry and told him his father was pretty cool.

One boy in his class, Dean Ando, said as an adult, "All I remember is Barry was just so happy that day it was incredible. What I remember most was the dad and Barry had the same smile. His dad was wearing this nice blue blazer, and he was nice to us."[6]

Barack, Sr., spent Christmas Day with his son, former wife, and in-laws. They posed for photographs by the family Christmas tree. Barry gave his father a necktie as a Christmas gift. Barack, Sr., gave Barry a basketball. The two spent considerable time together. Sometimes they spent time alone talking or reading side by side at home. One special activity they shared was a concert by jazz legend Dave Brubeck. Shortly after New Year's Day, however, Barack, Sr., flew back to Kenya.

Ann's marriage to Lolo followed a similar pattern to her marriage to Barack, Sr. She decided to stay in Hawaii and earn a master's degree in anthropology. Anthropology is the study of different cultures. Lolo stayed in Indonesia, and over time he and Ann drifted apart. The couple ended up getting divorced.

Meanwhile, Barry, Maya, and Ann moved into their own apartment. It was a small one but convenient for Barry. The new home was just a block away from Punahou School, and Barry could easily walk to class. Despite his rough beginning at Punahou, he gradually settled in. He made friends, and sometimes after school took them to the family apartment.

His classmate Bernice Bowers said that as time went on, "Barry was very good at making others around him

A Good Friend

One of Barry's best friends was Ray, an African American from Los Angeles. Ray was two years older than Barry. But as two of the few African-American students at Punahou, they had something in common. Ray moved to Hawaii because his father, a serviceman, was transferred there. The two became friends when Barry was fourteen.

> Barry found it offensive when people assumed things merely because of his skin color.

feel at ease while he himself was struggling with the rough and tumble of Punahou's very segmented, rigid social cliques."[7]

Many of Barry's classmates were from wealthy families. Sometimes they would complain to Barry how messy his apartment was, or how there was no food to snack on. In such a small apartment, it was easy for Barry's mother to overhear those comments. She often reminded Barry that she was both a single mother and a student and was doing the best she could.

Barry and his friend Ray would hang out, talk trash, and play basketball. While Barry never learned how to throw a decent spiral pass in football, he became a good basketball player. It was on the basketball courts that he met some of his closest friends, both white and African-American.

Then one day Barry's mother dropped a bombshell. She was moving back to Indonesia to do fieldwork. In anthropology, fieldwork is directly studying the people of a culture, as opposed to learning about them from books or articles. She wanted Barry to move to Indonesia with her and Maya. However, by now Barry felt comfortable in Hawaii. He chose to stay behind and live with Gramps and Toot.

About this time Barry began to feel caught between black and white worlds. Of course, first and foremost he was an individual. But when he heard racist jokes from people, he took them as personal insults. On the other hand, his friend Ray tended to see white people in general as racist. Yet Barry knew his grandparents were not like that.

He was offended when a white girl at school made a point to tell him how much she liked the African-American singer Stevie Wonder. He was just as offended when a white woman asked if he played basketball. Yet he did like Stevie Wonder and he did play basketball. But Barry found it offensive when people assumed things merely because of his skin color.

He decided to explore his heritage through African-American literature. That meant trips to the library where he took out books by some of the best-known African-American writers. These included James Baldwin, Richard Wright, Langston Hughes, and Ralph Ellison. Yet, Barry found them angry and frustrated in terms of their race.

Only one African-American author spoke to him. That was civil rights advocate Malcolm X. He was born Malcolm Little, but dropped his original last name since it was given to his ancestors by white slave owners. The letter "X" represented his long forgotten ancestral name. Malcolm was a member of the Nation of Islam, an American offshoot of the religion of Islam. He was a flamboyant leader who advocated African-American pride. But unlike Martin Luther King, Jr., Malcolm supported fighting violence with violence, and at times railed against white people. Barry related to Malcolm's African-American pride and insistence on respect but ignored his more militant ideals.[8]

Despite Barry's interest in African-American pride, his classmates did not notice any outwardly political side to him. Kelli Furushima, one of his classmates, later recalled, "He just seemed really laid back in school. He became political sometime afterward, because I did not see any hint of that in high school. . . . Except for one thing."[9]

That one thing was a poem Barry wrote. While many of his fellow students composed poems about familiar subjects such as school or sports, Barry chose a heavier topic.

The poem was called "The Old Man." It was written for the May 1979 issue of *Ka Wai Ola*, Punahou's literary journal. The journal name means "The Living Water." It refers to the fact that the school is said to be built over a sacred spring.

Barry's poem went like this:

> *I saw an old, forgotten man*
> *On an old, forgotten road.*
> *Staggering and numb under the glare of the*
> *Spotlight. His eyes, so dull and grey,*
> *Slide from right, to left, to right,*
> *Looking for his life, misplaced in a*
> *Shallow, muddy gutter long ago.*
> *I am found, instead.*
> *Seeking a hiding place, the night seals us together.*

A transient spark lights his face, and in my honor,
He pulls out forgotten dignity from under his flaking coat,
And walks a straight line along the crooked world.[10]

Aside from contributing to the school literary journal, Barry made the varsity basketball team. Bernice Bowers recalled, "Honestly, he got just a little cocky. It was the only time any of us saw him acting out the role of a cool basketball player. You could see him trying it [the attitude] on like a piece of clothing, but underneath it all he was still a good guy and the attitude didn't last too long."[11]

Bowers said that in addition to his extracurricular activities, Barry was a clear thinker and excellent writer. One time he spent his forty-five minute lunch period banging out a term paper on a school typewriter. It included material on political, social and economic trends. Bowers noted, "He had lots of natural abilities. When he just sat down and wrote the entire term paper in one sitting, I remember thinking, 'Oh my God, this guy is brilliant.'"[12]

Barry had by now lost touch with his father, Barack, Sr. But by the time Barry became a senior, his mother returned from her Indonesia fieldwork. So Barry moved out of his grandparents' place and in with Ann and Maya.

It was not long afterward that Ann noticed that Barry had developed some bad attitudes. Though Barry's grades were respectable, she did not think he was doing his best. She expected him to go to college, but Barry did not know if he wanted to.

WE GO PLAY HOOP

Thanks Tut, Gramps, Choom Gang, and Ray for all the good times.

Barry Obama

Obama in his 1979 senior portrait in the Punahou School yearbook. The photo on the left shows Obama playing basketball with an unidentified person. Below it, Obama thanks Tutu (who he calls Tut here), Gramps, and his good friend Ray, along with the "Choom Gang."

Ann was disturbed to learn that one of Barry's good friends was arrested for drug possession. What she may or may not have known is that Barry himself was now abusing drugs. He admits to smoking marijuana and using cocaine as a distraction from his questions about his racial identity.

He said, "I think it was typical of a teenager who was confused about who he was and what his place in the world was and thought experimenting with drugs was a way to rebel. It's not something that I'm proud of."[13]

Unlike his friend, Barry never got caught using drugs. He was also offered heroin, but he refused it. Barry spent the latter part of his senior year in high school applying to numerous colleges. Several accepted him. A small Los Angeles college named Occidental College offered him a full scholarship, so that is where he decided to go.

Shortly before leaving Hawaii, Barry had a conversation with an elderly African-American man. The man was a friend of Gramps. He was a published poet in his younger days. Barry grew to respect the man's wisdom. The youngster and old man chatted about Barry's decision to go to college.

The man asked Barry what he expected to get out of college. Barry answered that he did not know. The man did not seem surprised by Barry's reply. He said that a lot of young people go to college only because they feel that is the next thing they should do with their lives.

The man gave Barry one bit of advice. He told him not to lose his identity as a black man at a mostly white college. "You've got to go," he told Barry. "I'm just telling you to keep your eyes open. Stay awake."[14]

A few days later, Barry left for Los Angeles.

Chapter 4

"Not as Long as You Say It Right"

arry Obama arrived in Los Angeles in the fall of 1979. Tall and lanky with a short Afro haircut, Barry moved into a dormitory called Haines Hall. He soon started living the life of a typical college freshman. When not in class, he was often in his dorm room studying for exams, chowing down on pizza, blasting his stereo, or discussing political issues with other Haines Hall residents. He liked to let off steam in his leisure time playing basketball or driving around the city with friends.

College freshmen are required to take certain courses. But they can also choose courses called electives. Obama chose two. One was about American politics, starting with the Revolutionary War and continuing through the civil rights movement. The other covered modern European politics.

The professor who taught both classes was Roger Boesche. Boesche said that Obama was a thoughtful and curious student. He added, "You didn't take my European Modern class without wanting to think about deep ideas."[1]

Another professor who knew Obama was Eric Newhall. He teaches American studies and English. Newhall knew Obama not from the classroom but from the basketball court. He and Obama often took part in pickup games during their leisure time.

Newhall says, "You can tell a lot about a person's character in how they behave in that kind of situation. You can sense some things. He could talk a little smack, but Barack was a team player and a good passer. I could tell he paid attention to the people around him."[2]

Newhall jokes, "If he is elected president I'll be in the position to say I scored a good number of baskets against the President of the United States. Right now I have been saying I scored against the senator from Illinois."[3]

Deep down inside, Obama was trying to come to terms with his identity as half white and half African-American. He began to hang around mostly with African-American students. At one point, Obama was asked why he decided to be black rather than white. He answered, "I'm not sure I decided it. If you look African-American in this society, you're treated as an African-American, and when you're a child, in particular, that is how you begin to identify yourself."[4]

At college, he often came down hard on African Americans who did not appear to emphasize their race as he did. One time on campus he encountered a young woman named Joyce. Like Obama, she was also of mixed heritage. Her father was Italian and her mother was part African. Barry asked her if she was going to an upcoming meeting at the Black Student Association. She replied that she was not black but multiracial. She added that white people treated her with more respect than black people did. She commented that African Americans were always making her choose to be one race or the other. Barry was angry at Joyce's attitude. He thought she was being disloyal to her African-American roots.[5]

Another time he was chatting in a dormitory room with two African-American friends named Reggie and Marcus. Marcus was a strong believer in black pride. As they talked, another African-American student named Tim walked in the room to ask Barry about a homework assignment. According to Barry, Tim had little interest in his African-American culture or political issues.

After Tim left, Barry mocked him behind his back for not being a true African American. Reggie laughed, but surprisingly, the activist Marcus called Barry on it. Marcus said to Barry that he should mind his own business. He told Barry that Tim did not bother anyone. Marcus said that Barry should worry more about himself and not pass judgment on how other people should act.

Barry was angry at Marcus, but then realized Marcus was right.[6]

It was during Obama's sophomore, or second, year at Occidental that he became involved in a political cause.

Becoming Barack Again

One time, Barry was talking to his friend Marcus in a coffee shop when an African-American student named Regina joined them. She heard Marcus refer to Obama by his given name, Barack, instead of Barry. After Marcus left to go to class, Regina asked about the name Marcus called him. Obama replied that his real name was Barack. He explained that his father was Kenyan.

Regina responded by repeating his name. She said, "Barack. It's beautiful. So why does everyone call you Barry?"

Obama answered, "Habit, I guess. My father used it when he arrived in the States. I don't know whether that was his idea or somebody else's. He probably used Barry because it was easier to pronounce. You know—helped him fit in. Then it got passed onto me. So I could fit in."

Regina asked, "Do you mind if I call you Barack?"

Obama answered, "Not as long as you say it right."[7]

From then on, he became known more often as Barack and less often as Barry.

The nation of South Africa practiced a policy called apartheid. The country was run by a white minority that practiced legal racism against the black African majority. Apartheid was similar to the segregation practiced in the American South for many decades. However, by 1980 South Africa was one of the few nations in the world with such a policy.

Many wanted South Africa to end apartheid. They felt one way to accomplish this was to encourage colleges and businesses to stop doing business with South Africa. If that happened, then South Africa would lose money. If the South African government banned apartheid, the colleges and businesses would resume doing business with them. This policy is called divestment.

Obama first joined the divestment movement at Occidental as a way of showing his friends that he was a proud and strong African American. But the more time he spent at meetings, the more involved he became in the movement. He helped organize rallies, write letters, and contact speakers to come and talk to students. He also practiced debating and found that people listened to his opinions.

Obama was asked by other members of the divestment movement to be the opening speaker at an outdoor rally. His speech was to be part of a staged performance. After he spoke several opening sentences, two students dressed as South African soldiers were to pull him offstage.

Barack Obama spoke out against apartheid in South Africa.
Above, people distribute propaganda books against apartheid in
Johannesburg, South Africa, in 1985.

Obama would struggle to break free of them. The act was to be a symbol of the lack of free speech in South Africa.

The whole thing went according to plan. However, as the students were dragging Obama off the stage, he found that he did not want to leave. He wanted to keep talking to the crowd. He did leave the stage as planned, though, and relinquished it to other speakers.

His old basketball friend, Professor Eric Newhall, said, "I saw an authentic social commitment on his part, as opposed to being fake or phony. Some students are [only] politically active until they graduate. So it doesn't surprise me that he is a presidential candidate."[8]

After his sophomore year at Occidental, Obama decided to attend a different college. He was happy at Occidental, but felt it did not give him a worldly outlook. Los Angeles is a big city, but Occidental is a little college located in a residential neighborhood. Obama wanted a bigger city experience, so he transferred to Columbia University in New York City. Obama said, "Because Occidental was so small, I felt that I had gotten what I needed out of it and the idea of being in New York was very appealing."[9]

Every college student must major in one subject. That means he or she takes more courses in that subject than any other. The goal is to get a job in that field after graduation. Obama majored in political science, the study of government and politics. The part of political science that he liked most was international relations, the governments, and politics of other countries.

Obama was unable to get a dormitory room on the Columbia campus. So he arranged to live in a city apartment near the college. But his first night in New York did not go as he planned. When he arrived at the apartment a little after 10 o'clock at night, no one was there to let him in. He did not have enough money to stay in a motel, so he ended up sleeping outdoors in an alleyway.

Columbia University, where Obama attended, is highly regarded and was founded in 1754 as King's College. Above is the university's library building.

The next day he looked up an acquaintance he met in Los Angeles who had moved to New York. His name was Sadik. Although he was of Pakistani origin, Sadik was from London, England. He had moved to the United States two years earlier. Sadik showed Obama around the city and the two became friends. Obama was able to move into his apartment, but soon left it because of poor heating. He and Sadik decided to rent an apartment together.

Columbia University is located on the outskirts of a mostly African-American neighborhood called Harlem. When Obama had spare time, he liked to shoot baskets in a Harlem park. He attended services at a neighborhood Baptist church, and became involved in the college's Black Students Organization. As at Occidental, Obama took part in anti-apartheid rallies. Mostly, he spent time in his apartment studying.

He said, "When I transferred, I decided to buckle down and get serious. I spent a lot of time in the library. I didn't socialize that much. I was like a monk."[10]

When Sadik wanted to go out for fun, Obama often stayed home and studied. Once after Obama turned down yet another offer from his roommate, Sadik told Obama he was becoming a bore.

However, Obama did not change his routine. In addition to taking his studies very seriously, he paid more attention to his health. He quit using drugs and ran three miles a day for exercise. He also fasted every Sunday.

After his junior, or third, year of college, Obama took a summer job working at a construction site in the city. That summer he had some special guests. His mother, Ann, and half-sister Maya arrived in New York to visit him. Barry was busy with his job so Ann and Maya spent their days by themselves seeing sights like the Metropolitan Museum of Art and the Statue of Liberty.

Barack Obama's half-sister, Maya Soetoro-Ng, visited him while he attended Columbia University in New York. Here, she laughs during a spiritual rally in Honolulu on June 24, 2007.

At night they all met for dinner. Ann and Maya would tell Barack about the places they saw that day. Barack would listen patiently. Then he would discuss politics with them. Sometimes it seemed that he was lecturing rather than taking part in a discussion. He often told them about the problems of the poor in the city. He even told his mother that the business dealings of the place she worked were unfair to poor people in other countries.

One day during her visit, Ann saw that Barack was holding a letter addressed to his father. He told his mother that he was planning to visit Barack, Sr., in Kenya after he graduated from college in a year. She encouraged the trip and hoped Barack would get to know his father better.

Obama had not seen his father since he was ten. He imagined his father as a big-shot economist in the Kenyan government. In Obama's mind, his father had a nice office and had many clerks and secretaries working under him. Obama figured other economists often called his father for advice.

The trip never took place, though. A few months after Ann and Maya returned to Hawaii, Barack received the news that his father had died in a car accident. Barack did not go to his father's funeral in Kenya, but he did write a letter to his father's family offering his sympathy. With his father dead, Barack felt there was no rush to make the long trip to Kenya.

Obama spent much of his senior year thinking about what kind of job he wanted to take after college. He knew one thing: He wanted to do something that would make a difference in people's lives. Obama graduated from Columbia in the spring of 1983. It was time to start a path to a career. But what path would that be?

Chapter 5

The World
of Business

Obama decided to stay in New York City and find a job as a community organizer. Community organizers help people mainly in poor neighborhoods identify and fix problems. These can include poor housing, gang violence, not enough jobs, and a lack of worthwhile activities for young people to keep them from getting into trouble. Community organizers get people in these neighborhoods together to discuss possible solutions. Then they put their efforts into making those solutions work.

By working with the residents of poor neighborhoods directly, community organizers are working from the bottom up. That is, they are not dealing with the government or big businesses that would in turn start job programs to help the poor. They work with those who would be the recipients of such programs. They are often compared to the roots of grass. It is from the roots that grass grows. So these organizers are said to work in grassroots organizations.

Nobody will get rich being a community organizer. The job is generally low paying. People who take this type of job do so because they think the help they give others is more important than making a lot of money.

One reason Obama decided to become a community organizer was because of the politics of the United States at that time. Ronald Reagan, a conservative Republican, was president of the United States. Conservative Republicans generally believe that government programs are not good for poor people.

Some government programs give poor people money to help them pay their bills. This system is called welfare. Those who support welfare believe poor people need that money to get on their feet. Then once they get jobs they no longer need welfare. Conservative Republicans oppose the idea of welfare since they believe it makes people rely on the government for money. They tend to think that when people use the government for money it makes them less interested in getting jobs.

Welfare money comes from people's taxes, and conservative Republicans feel that is not fair to taxpayers. They also believe that by not working, welfare recipients are not contributing to society. They feel the best way for the poor to get ahead is to get a job, even if it is a low-paying one. Then after gaining experience, they can get better and higher-paying jobs.

Reagan's critics were mostly liberal Democrats. They felt that the wealthy would not create new jobs with their tax cuts. The liberals believed the wealthy would either keep the money or spend it on luxury items for themselves.

President Ronald Reagan

Ronald Reagan was the strongest conservative Republican president since the 1920s. While his supporters felt his anti-government-programs idea was good for the country, his opponents thought his ideas hurt people who had nowhere else to go for money to live on. They felt if it were not for government-welfare programs, the poor would not have food to eat or a place to live.

Reagan also believed in giving tax cuts to some of the nation's wealthiest people. Reagan's idea was not to make the rich richer. He believed his policy would allow wealthy people to make their businesses bigger and more profitable. That would create more jobs, which in turn would help the poor.

Obama was against Reagan's conservative policies and became a community organizer to work against them.

These people felt that under Reagan the poor were getting poorer and the rich were getting richer. Some even felt that Reagan's policies glorified rich people and hurt the poor.

Obama was a liberal and a strong critic of Reagan's policies. He believed he had to work with the poor directly to help them counter what he saw as Reagan's negative policies.

Obama wrote letters to civil rights organizations across the country. He told them about his education and discussed how qualified he was to work for them. He also wrote the same letters to elected African-American officials and small groups across the country that helped specific neighborhoods. The problem was that none seemed to want to hire him. No matter how many letters he sent out, he never received any responses.

Rather than give up, Obama decided to postpone his search for work as a community organizer. He decided to take a more traditional job for a year. He could use the money to pay back loans he took out for his college education. Maybe he could even start putting money into a savings account.

Obama was hired to work for a company called Business International Corporation, known by the initials BI. BI is a consulting company for American businesses located overseas. That means BI consults with, or gives

As a businessman and a community organizer, Obama learned to deal with and talk to people. Above, Obama shakes hands with ten-year-old Donovan Dodds as Obama leaves a presidential-campaign rally on April 14, 2007.

advice to, these businesses on ways they could be more efficient and productive.

Obama's job was research assistant. He helped others find information about BI's projects. Every day Obama went to the BI main office in the middle of New York City. He wore a suit and tie and carried a briefcase to work.

Obama was the only African-American male at BI. That fact bothered him.[1]

However, African-American women who worked at BI as secretaries were proud of him. They told him that someday he would run the whole company. But Obama was happy telling them how much he looked forward to working in the future as a community organizer.

One African American critical of Obama's future plans was a man named Ike. He worked as a security guard at BI. Ike told Obama he should forget those plans and take a job where he could earn some good money. He told Obama that he had a good speaking voice and could be a successful television announcer. Ike said that working as a community organizer was a waste of time. Ike added that poor people who want to achieve something will find a way to do it. He added that those who do not make an effort to improve their lives would not appreciate his attempts to help them.

> They told Obama that someday he would run the whole company.

At first, Obama brushed off Ike's advice. He stuck to his dream. Yet, after serving several months at BI, Obama started thinking that maybe Ike was right.

For one thing, Obama was promoted from research assistant to financial writer. As part of his new job, Obama interviewed important businesspeople from countries such as Japan and Germany. He was given his own office and a personal secretary. The money was rolling in. Obama started to wonder if this was where his future was—the world of business.

One day Obama was at work ready to write an article on financial matters when he received a surprise phone call. On the other end of the phone was his half-sister Auma. She had left Kenya and was living in Germany to attend college. She told Obama that she and some friends planned to visit the United States in a few weeks. She wanted to finally meet her half brother. Obama was delighted and told her she could stay with him in New York.

Obama spent the next several weeks on a shopping spree buying things like bedsheets, bath towels, and kitchenware to make Auma's visit more comfortable. However, she never made it to the United States.

Two days before she was to arrive in New York, she called Obama again. This time the news was bad. She began crying as she said that one of their brothers, David, had just died in a motorcycle accident. Her trip to the United States was canceled. Maybe she could make a trip some-time in the future. Instead, she would be flying home to Kenya for her brother's funeral.

Obama had never met David, and did not make the long flight to Kenya. However, David's death affected him very strongly. He began to think more about life in general and what he wanted to do with his own life. He concluded that he wanted to do more than make a lot of money working for a consulting company. Barack Obama wanted to do something more personal. He wanted a job where he could directly help people. He had no problem taking a pay cut to do so. He decided again to follow his dream and become a community organizer.

A few months after receiving Auma's phone call, Obama took the first step in starting a new life. He quit his job at BI and applied for community organizing jobs. As before, he had trouble at first finding anyone who wanted to hire him. Still, he did not quit.

Obama finally received a job offer from a well-established civil rights group in New York. His main responsibility would be to help organize conferences on issues that concern poor, inner-city residents. These included decent housing, employment, and drug abuse.

During the job interview Obama learned that he would be working out of an office. This civil rights group worked closely with the government and private business-es to reach its goals. That part of the job did not interest Obama. He wanted to work directly with poor people. Although he needed employment, he turned it down.

So Obama went back to looking for the type of work he had his heart set on doing. To help pay bills over the next six months, he worked odd jobs around the city. When he was about to give up on his dream, Obama received a phone call from a community organizer in

Chicago. He was a white man named Gerald Kellman who was interested in hiring Obama as a trainee. Kellman told Obama he would be flying to New York the next week and the two could meet then.

When they met, Kellman told Obama he was looking for someone to help people find jobs in the mostly African-American Southside of Chicago. Many companies that ran factories in the area had closed. Those that did not close were employing fewer and fewer people. Kellman needed someone to start job-placement centers and training centers to help former factory workers find new work. Since the neighborhood in question was African-American, Kellman felt it was important to hire an African American for that job.

> Obama was also given two thousand dollars to buy a car.

Obama joked, "They didn't have a lot of money. So all they could afford was me."[2]

The starting salary was low: ten thousand dollars a year. People in businesses such as the computer industry could start out making three or four times that amount at that time. Obama was also given two thousand dollars to buy a car.[3] He could buy a used car with that amount of money, but certainly not a new car. It did not matter to Obama. When Kellman offered him the job, Obama was thrilled to take it. He was ready to put all his energy into empowering the poor, but he needed the guidance of someone experienced such as Kellman.

Kellman said, "He wanted to make that kind of contribution and didn't know how to do it. There's that side of him that's strongly idealistic, very much a dreamer, and this kind of work attracts that kind of person. It isn't just that we're going to change things, but we're going to change things from the grass roots."[4]

Soon after his meeting with Kellman, Obama packed up his belongings in his car and drove to Chicago.

Chapter 6

The
Organizer

After Obama arrived in Chicago and made himself at home, Kellman told him that he would be working with two organizations. They were made up mostly of members of churches in some of the city's poorest areas. Churches have always played a major role in organizing efforts in African-American communities. During the civil rights movement, Martin Luther King, Jr., based most of his efforts out of African-American churches.

One of the Chicago organizations Obama would work with was the Calumet Community Religious Conference (CCRC). It consisted of twenty Chicago-area churches. The other was a group of eight churches. It was the Developing Communities Project (DCP).

When traveling through these neighborhoods, Obama saw dilapidated houses, decrepit and vacant storefronts, and teenagers hanging idly around on the streets. One would think the people he spoke with would be thrilled to find someone interested in helping them out. Yet many wanted nothing to do with him. They felt that they had been used and lied to before by others who had said they wanted to help. That included politicians and business leaders. The residents felt that in the end these so-called helpers did not want to help the poor as much as they wanted to use them for votes or a better public image.

One person who signed up to work with Obama was Loretta Augustine-Herron. She said of the neighborhoods where Obama would work, "It was poverty on top of

Barack Obama began his political career in the city of Chicago.

poverty. There were so many people who had given up. They just didn't care. I don't think he knew how bad it was until he came to our area."[1]

Some may have given up, but not Obama. He got busy in a housing project called Altgeld Gardens. In spite of the name, there were no gardens on the grounds. The complex consisted of two thousand two-story brick apartments. Across the street was a smelly sewage treatment plant. Like others on Chicago's Southside, the residents of Altgeld Gardens had heard time and time again that people wanted to help them. Yet, the results were always the same; nothing happened to improve their lives. No wonder they were discouraged.

At one point Obama and some coworkers were looking over a brochure from the Mayor's Office of Employment and Training (MOET). The purpose of the MOET was to help train unemployed people for new jobs. While reading the MOET brochure, Obama noticed there were no MOET programs listed in Chicago's Southside.

Obama and his staff wrote a letter to a woman named Cynthia Alvarez, the director of MOET. In the letter they stressed the need for MOET programs and a job-training center in the Southside. A meeting between Alvarez and residents of Altgeld Gardens took place two weeks later. As a result, Alvarez promised that MOET would open a job-placement center in the neighborhood within six months.

His Father's Real Fate

The political situation in Kenya had gotten unstable and corrupt while Obama's father lived there. Many Kenyan businessmen refused to question the government. However, Obama's father spoke out. He wanted to know why he was passed over for promotions. He soon earned the reputation as a troublemaker. That was enough to get him fired. When Barack, Sr.'s reputation as a problem worker got out, it was hard for him to find another job.

The only work he could find was a small job at the water department. It was a huge step down in his career. Discouraged, Barack, Sr., began to drink heavily and became abusive towards his family.[2] His wife finally left him. He was then fired from his job with the water department. Without work, he had little money. The family had to move to a ramshackle house in a tough neighborhood.

Finally, a new government took over in Kenya. It made changes for the better and Barack, Sr., was hired back into the government. Yet Auma said her father never got over his bitterness. The family never became a close one again.

Shortly afterward, Obama's half-sister Auma made the visit to the United States she had postponed after their brother had died. As the two spent time together, Auma told Obama details about their father's life. Obama learned through Auma that his father was not the bigwig economist he had imagined. Barack, Jr., was brokenhearted to learn the reality about the father he had thought so highly of.[3]

Obama could put the truths about his father in the back of his mind. He dedicated himself to working hard with the residents of Altgeld Gardens. While some seemed to be without hope, others did work closely together with Obama to improve their living situations. There were true successes. After a year, Obama and his staff were able to organize neighborhood cleanups, sponsor career days for young people, and cooperate with local government officials to improve sanitation services. They also met with the city's parks department to make area parks safer and more attractive. Another positive change was the start of neighborhood crime-watch programs.

Before long, Obama became aware of a very serious health situation. He learned that the mineral asbestos was used in the construction of an office building at Altgeld Gardens. At one

> Before long, Obama became aware of a very serious health situation.

time asbestos was commonly used in buildings because it is resistant to fire. However, scientists later learned that asbestos can also cause illnesses, including cancer. Consequently, the use of asbestos was banned in many places.

When residents of Altgeld Gardens learned that asbestos was found in an office building in their housing complex, they wondered if it was also in their personal apartments. Obama helped organize a meeting between Altgeld residents and their housing manager. When they did not get the answers they wanted, Obama took several tenants directly to the Chicago Housing Authority (CHA). The CHA is in charge of making sure all public housing in Chicago is safe.

When they asked to see the director of the CHA, a receptionist told them he was not in his office. She told them to talk to the housing manager at Altgeld Gardens. An Altgeld resident said they had already done so and they did not get an answer. The receptionist told the group to leave or she would call security and have them forcibly removed.

Just then, the elevator doors near the office opened. A group of television reporters and camera people poured out. The local television news departments had found out about the asbestos scare and felt it was important enough to cover.

Children walk alongside the Altgeld Gardens housing project in Chicago. Obama helped its residents fight asbestos contamination. The project is near steel mills, which for decades turned the night sky orange with pollution.

As soon as the reporters began asking questions about asbestos in Altgeld Gardens apartments, the CHA director's assistant ran out of her office to talk to them. While the director's assistant could easily tell Obama and the Altgeld residents to leave, she could not do so to the newspeople. After all, they were photographing her. Anything she said or did in front of the cameras would end up on the local nightly news.

With the cameras in her face, the director's assistant had no choice but to admit that no tests to find asbestos had yet been conducted at the apartments. She further promised that testing for asbestos would start by the end of the day. It was an important victory for Obama and those who worked with him.

After over three years working with the people of south Chicago, Obama made a daring decision. He decided to quit his job to go to Harvard Law School in Cambridge, Massachusetts.

He said, "At a certain point I realized—although the best education I ever received was the three years I worked in those low income neighborhoods—I realized I needed to learn more to be more effective. So I went to law school."[4]

> "I realized I needed to learn more to be more effective. So I went to law school."

Some of the people he worked with were concerned that Obama would forget about them. They feared that after he graduated from law school he would take a job for a powerful law firm so he could make a lot of money. Obama assured them he would be back.

Shortly before he moved, Obama attended a service at the Trinity United Church of Christ in his neighborhood. In his sermon at that service, the Reverend Jeremiah A. Wright, Jr., spoke at length about hardships people constantly face. He discussed problems such as world hunger

The original Trinity United Church of Christ, where
Barack Obama first attended services in 1988, stands a few blocks
down the street from the new structure.

and discrimination. Wright cited biblical passages to underscore his points.

But Wright added that there is always a bright side. He described the positive way of looking at troubles as "the audacity of hope." That phrase was so important that Wright titled the sermon "The Audacity of Hope." The word "audacity" means being daring or bold.

According to Obama, Wright said in his sermon:

> Look, it's easy to be cynical. It is easy to despair, because there's so much evidence of hardship and heartbreak and war and famine all across the world and in our own communities, and oftentimes hardships in our own lives. But what is truly audacious, what takes risk and boldness, is to hope.[5]

Obama added, "And I always loved that idea, because I think it's true."[6] Obama would remember that sermon for the rest of his life.

Chapter 7

His Father's Past and His Own Future

Before he moved to Massachusetts to begin law school, Obama made a pilgrimage. His destination was the place of his father's heritage: Kenya. There he would spend four weeks exploring his roots.

Obama spent the first leg of his trip visiting his half sister Auma. The two walked around the Kenyan capital, Nairobi. One of the first things Obama noticed was a clash of cultures.

In some ways, Nairobi was like any city. Obama saw high-rise office buildings, classy hotels, and luxury car dealerships. But as Obama stood in front of a dealership selling expensive Mercedes-Benzes, he noticed a group of

Granny's Story of British Oppression

Granny was old enough to remember when settlers and missionaries came from Britain to colonize her homeland. They set up missions to convert Kenyans to Christianity. British colonizers put a tax on the huts the Kenyans called their homes. Those Kenyans who did not pay taxes had their huts burned to the ground by the British. Native Kenyans were drafted into the British colonial military service. Kenyans who fought back were beaten or shot. It is no wonder that the Kenyans called the British colonizers *Bwana Ogalo*, or "the oppressor."[1]

Senator Barack Obama (right) claps hands with his grandmother, Sarah Hussein Obama, in Kenya on August 26, 2006. He also visited his grandmother shortly before he attended law school.

women that walked past. The women had altered their bodies to fit in with the traditions of the Masai tribe. Their heads were shaved. Their earlobes were unnaturally long and covered with colorful beads. It was clear to Obama that he was no longer in the United States.

After touring the city, Auma took Obama to visit relatives he had never met. There were half brothers, aunts and uncles, nieces and nephews, and his father's mother. Obama's time with his grandmother, Sarah Hussein Obama, who he and Auma called Granny, was among his most rewarding in Kenya.

Granny told Obama that his grandfather, Onyango, learned to live under British colonial rule. Through additional conversations with his grandmother, Obama learned more about both his grandfather and father.

For one thing, the two did not have a close relationship. Onyango had little faith that Barack's father would ever amount to anything. For awhile they did not talk to one another.

Obama also learned that his father was married before he married Obama's mother. When he was only eighteen, Obama's father married a Kenyan girl named Kezia. Kezia gave birth to a son named Roy before giving birth to Auma. Obama's father left his wife and children behind to attend the University of Hawaii. It was there that Obama's father met and married Obama's mother, Ann. Polygamy, or having more than one wife, was a traditional Kenyan practice.

Malik Obama, Barack's older half-brother, holds a picture of Barack (left), himself (middle), and an unidentified friend in Kenya on September 14, 2004. The photo was most likely taken when Obama visited Kenya before law school.

Whether Ann knew about Barack, Sr.'s other family in Kenya is unclear.

Obama also learned from Granny that at Harvard, Barack, Sr., began dating another woman. He left her in Massachusetts to return to Kenya. But she followed him to Kenya where they were married. It is not known whether Barack, Sr., officially divorced Kezia, but he had little to do with her afterward. After hearing these stories, Obama walked to the nearby gravesites of his father and grandfather and wept.

Filled with a new understanding of his family, Obama flew back to the United States. He started law school at Harvard in the fall of 1988. Law school is a huge commitment. It takes three years of constant and intense studying to graduate.

Obama had matured. He was no longer the slacker that he had been at Occidental College. He worked hard and said he spent his time "doing the things that we tell ourselves we finally must do to grow up."[2] While Obama spent much of his time in classrooms, he spent just as much time in Harvard's libraries. There he stayed for hours at a time, studying old law cases and rulings.

Some of the cases were encouraging, such as *Brown* v. *Board of Education*. That was the name of the 1954 ruling by the United States Supreme Court that outlawed segregation in public schools. Yet Obama said that for every case like *Brown*, there were plenty where justice did not prevail. Still, he was hopeful that in the end, the right thing would always be done.

After his first year of law school was completed, Obama returned to Chicago for the summer. To gain experience, he spent those hot months working as an intern at a law firm. His advisor was a lawyer named

> Obama and
> Robinson got
> along well
> and decided
> to meet
> for lunch.

Michelle Robinson. She had also attended Harvard Law School.

Robinson's background was very different from Obama's. Like Obama, she is an African American. But she grew up on Chicago's Southside. Her father was a city worker, and the family never had a lot of money. She said that getting pizza on a Friday night was a splurge, and going to the circus once a year was a big deal.

Despite their differences, Robinson says they have common roots beyond race. She notes, "Really, though, we're both Midwesterners. Underneath it all, he's very Kansas, because of his grandparents and his mom."[3]

Obama and Robinson got along well and decided to meet for lunch outside the office. Soon they were dating. When summer was over, Obama returned to Harvard, but the couple stayed in touch.

Obama's grades during law school were so good that he was allowed to run for a special position: president of the Harvard Law Review. A law review is an organization at a college or university that publishes a journal, also called a law review. The journal is filled with articles about legal issues written by both professors and students. Only the best students can be a part of a law review. Also, it is time-consuming, requiring intense reading and writing to stay a part of it.

Being president of a law review is an additional responsibility. But those who succeed are almost assured of good-paying jobs after graduation. Of all the college or university law reviews, Harvard's is one of the most respected. The law review's editors are responsible for voting for its president.

A total of nineteen candidates ran for the honor. The editors eliminated several contestants soon afterward. The race finally came down to a choice between two candidates: Barack Obama and a young man named David Goldberg. When the final vote was taken, Obama was the winner.

Obama has strong liberal views. One classmate and fellow law review member, Bradford Berenson, is a conservative. Berenson said that Obama's success stemmed in large part to his ability to get along with those who disagreed with his views. According to Berenson, "There was a lot of interpersonal conflict and hostility and bitterness between the liberals and conservatives on the law review. We could count on Obama to have an open mind and take conservatives' views into account."[4]

At first, Berenson supported another candidate for law review president. But when the election came down to a two-person race between Obama and Goldberg, Berenson favored Obama. Berenson stressed, "Obama was a little older than the other students, and had more life experience. That allowed him to put aside a lot of the petty political conflicts."[5]

Berenson continued, "He [Obama] was affable and relaxed, and projected a certain aura of cool. As president of the law review, he was generally in the role of peacemaker with the different factions."[6]

Berenson did criticize Obama to a degree. "As much as Barack is seriously interested in hearing views from others who disagree with him, I think he never seems to adjust these views in regards to his own positions. He has always had a liberal voting record. Yet there is a great value in feeling you've been heard, that someone has listened to you."[7]

On the other hand, Obama had to deal with liberal views he rejected. Some African-American students wanted special treatment. They said it was only right since the legal field was prejudiced against African Americans. They believed that the only way they could achieve success was by being given a special boost. Conservatives strongly disagreed with that idea. They felt any person should be given assignments or jobs based only on their skills. At times the two sides were at each other's throats.

Berenson said, "I have worked in the Supreme Court and the White House and I never saw politics as bitter as at Harvard Law Review in the early '90s." The two sides were so ardent, he added, that they would boo and hiss one another in class.[8]

Obama was the first African-American president of the Harvard Law Review. However, he did not turn the law review into a sounding board only for issues important to African Americans. A conservative journalist, Carol Platt Liebau, wrote that:

> More radical black Review editors urged him not only to take controversial stands on a whole host of racial issues—they also pressured him to use his discretion to elevate black students to leadership positions within the organization. Barack declined to do so; though his choices were often left-wing (as, in fairness, was much of the Review's membership), they weren't race-conscious.[9]

Obama proved he was not only an able student and leader, but also a man with a sense of humor. In a parody of the law review published by Harvard students, Obama wrote a fake biography about himself. It read in part, "I was born in Oslo, Norway, the son of a Volvo factory worker and part-time ice fisherman. My mother was a backup singer for Abba. They were good folks. (In Chicago) I discovered I was black, and I have remained so ever since."[10]

As the review's first African-American president, Obama got national attention. A publisher signed him to write his memoirs. In addition, African-American actor Blair Underwood had been cast to play a

"(In Chicago), I discovered I was black, and I have remained so ever since."

lawyer on a new television drama, *L.A. Law*. When Underwood needed background detail for his role, he visited Obama to get information.

Obama graduated from law school in 1991. A fellow law student, Hill Harper, said that with Obama's education and experience, he could have easily had a job that would make him instantly rich. Harper added, "But he was committed to doing the work he wanted to do."[9] That meant going back to Chicago and working with the city's poor.

Obama was hired by the law firm of Miner, Barnhill & Galland. Miner, Barnhill & Galland deals mainly with victims of discrimination. Obama worked on cases involving voting rights, poor people's housing problems, and discrimination in the workplace.

Judson H. Miner, his employer, said about Obama:

> I was the first person to meet him. Obviously he had the credentials to work here, with the Harvard Law Review and all. He was obviously a very bright guy, a very personable fellow, a very thoughtful man. He was very much interested in working with the types of cases we handle here.[11]

Miner also said, "He was so talented that I think it was reasonably clear early on that he was going to be under a lot of pressure at some point to jump into government or politics."[12]

Before he was hired, Obama had already made two commitments. One was to finish his memoirs. The other was to serve as executive director of an effort called Illinois Project Vote.

Judson H. Miner said, "He [Obama] wasn't the kind of person to spend half his time working on other projects when he was supposed to be working for us. He proposed that he not start working for us until he finished those commitments since it wouldn't have been fair to us. So we let him do so."[13]

Obama's role for Illinois Project Vote included traveling up and down the state trying to register voters. By the time he was finished, Obama had helped register one hundred fifty thousand new voters in Illinois. Political experts have said that helped Bill Clinton carry Illinois in the 1992 presidential election.[14]

It was also in 1992 that Obama and Michelle Robinson were married. The wedding took place at Trinity United Church of Christ. Reverend Jeremiah A. Wright, Jr., conducted the ceremony. He was the same minister who a few years earlier had delivered the sermon titled "The Audacity of Hope" that Obama liked so much.

Obama said about his wedding day, "And for that moment, at least, I felt like the luckiest man alive."[15]

Obama settled into a routine. In addition to practicing law at Miner, Barnhill & Galland, he took a part-time job teaching at the University of Chicago Law School. On Tuesday, Thursday, and Friday mornings he, Michelle, and a businessman friend named Peter Byno worked out

Michelle Obama speaks during a fundraising event on March 9, 2007, in New York. She married Barack Obama in 1992.

in a Chicago gym. Obama still liked to play basketball whenever he could. But Byno said that when it came to basic exercises, Michelle showed them all up.

Byno said, "After an hour, Barack and I are crying for mercy and Michelle is still doing sit-ups, still on the treadmill, sort of laughing at us."[16]

In the summer of 1995, Obama's memoir was published. It was titled, *Dreams from My Father*. The book is over four hundred pages long. In it, Obama tells about his confusion over his racial identity. He begins the book by discussing his father's ancestors. He ends it by discussing the trip to Kenya he took just before beginning law school.

Sales of the book were mediocre, but the reviews were mostly positive. However, some have criticized Obama's practice of using composite characters. While the family members he discusses are all real, other characters are fictionalized versions of people he interacted with in his life.

By 1996, Obama was ready for another challenge. Like his previous ones, this would not be easy.

Chapter 8

In the Footsteps of Lincoln

I n 1996 Barack Obama decided to quit practicing law and run for political office.

The ground floor for many who want to get into politics is their state's legislature. So Obama decided to run for a seat in the Illinois State Senate. He would represent the same part of Chicago where he worked as a community organizer. If he was elected, he would play a role in making laws that would be in effect in the state of Illinois.

Friends and neighbors were not sure that Obama was making the correct decision. Obama said:

> People would ask me, 'You seem like a nice guy, you're a church-going man, got a wonderful law degree, great future ahead of you, why in the heck

would you want to go into something dirty and nasty like politics?' But I tell people the reason I got into politics is the same reason that people decided to form unions. And that is that we are all connected as one people. . . . If there is a child on the South Side of Chicago that can't read, that makes a difference in my life, even if it's not my child.[1]

Obama was new at campaigning. He decided the best way to be successful at this new task was to follow the example of others before him. He said, "After discussing it with my wife, I entered the race and proceeded to do what every first-time candidate does: I talked to anyone who would listen. I went to block club meetings and church socials, beauty shops and barbershops. If two guys were standing on a corner, I would cross the street to hand them campaign literature."[2]

Those techniques worked. Obama won the election. He officially took office early in 1997 in the Illinois state capital of Springfield. Then he went to work right away in the state capital building. It was not far from the Old State Capitol building, where Abraham Lincoln once held the same position.

Just as at the Harvard Law Review, Obama used diplomatic skills to work with both liberal Democrats and conservative Republicans. Unlike at Harvard, in Illinois the liberal Democrats were in the minority. The governor, Jim Edgar, was a Republican. The majority of the Illinois state legislature was Republican. Obama knew he had his work cut out for him. But he used his charm, patience, and tolerance to make friends with his opponents.

One of Obama's first successes was the first major ethics law passed in Illinois in twenty-five years. Another law he helped pass required that police videotape all interrogations and confessions in cases involving murder. Since some people who had been convicted of murder were later found to be innocent, Obama wanted to make sure that evidence in murder cases was as reliable as possible. He was willing to work with police to make the law fair. When police said the original bill was so restricting that it would hurt investigations, Obama modified it.

A Republican's View of Obama

Republican Kirk Dillard had been a state senator for four years when Obama was elected. Dillard said, "I knew from the day he walked into this chamber that he was destined for great things. In Republican circles, we've always feared that Barack would become a rock star of American politics."[3]

Dillard added, "Senator Obama was someone who I thought—and I was right—could tackle extremely complex things like ethics reform, the death penalty, or racial profiling by law enforcement."[4] Ethics reform is changing rules to make sure that office holders act in the best interests of the people.

Obama would prove Dillard right.

Barack Obama stands outside the Illinois Senate chambers
during his time as a state senator.

Obama was named the chairman of the State Senate's Health and Human Services Committee. In that role, he helped pass laws giving low-income families better access to health care. He also helped get more money for AIDS prevention and care programs.

As much as he could be diplomatic with opponents, he did not hesitate to hit hard when necessary. Once during a senate session, a Republican senator blasted a plan that would provide breakfasts to preschool-aged children. Obama said that the Republican senator said the program "would crush their [the preschoolers] spirit of self-reliance. I had to point out that not too many five-year-olds I knew were self-reliant, but children who spent their formative years too hungry to learn could very well end up being charges of the state."[5]

Although Obama fought hard for that bill, it was defeated. However, an adapted version of it did pass later.

There was an addition to the Obama family in 1999. Michelle gave birth to a daughter she and Obama named Malia. It was a time for many changes in Obama's life. In addition to becoming a father, Obama decided he was ready to make a major leap in his career. Satisfied with the way he represented the people of his district for the state of Illinois, he decided to try for a position on a bigger stage: the United States Congress. He wanted to represent his neighborhood and the rest of the state of Illinois's first congressional district in Washington.

To be the Democratic candidate for Congress, he first had to earn his party's nomination. Only then could he run in the general election against the Republican nominee.

The incumbent, or sitting congressman, was also a Democrat. His name was Bobby Rush. Obama would have to face Rush in a primary election to be the Democratic nominee.

Experienced politicians had warned Obama not to challenge Rush. Rush was a former member of an activist African-American organization called the Black Panthers. The Panthers were formed in 1965 and were active in the late 1960s and early 1970s. They promoted black pride, civil rights, and self-defense for African Americans.

The Black Panthers took part in community programs to fight poverty, hunger, and illness in the African-American community. While some whites as well as most African Americans supported those ideas, many had a negative opinion of the Black Panthers. One reason was because they felt that the call for self-defense was an excuse to use violence.

But in the year 2000, the Black Panthers no longer existed as a group. Rush, however, was a fixture in Chicago's African-American community. He was working to change things from a position within the government. In 1999, Rush helped pass the Nursing Relief for Disadvantaged Areas Act. There had been a nursing shortage in his district. Rush's bill helped reduce the shortage by allowing qualified foreign nurses to work in Chicago by providing them with visas, official documents they need to live in and travel in the United States.

Despite Rush's legacy, Dan Shomon, who managed Obama's campaign, was optimistic about Obama's chances. Shomon said, "A lot of people were frustrated with the incumbent and came to Barack and asked him to run."[6]

Obama's run for Congress turned out to be a total disaster. In a poll taken two weeks after Obama announced his candidacy, a total of 90 percent of the people said they recognized Rush's name. Only 11 percent recognized Obama's.[7]

> Rush . . . exploited the differences in his and Obama's backgrounds for his own good.

Rush was a shrewd campaigner. He exploited the differences in his and Obama's backgrounds for his own good. Rush noted that Obama grew up in Hawaii and attended expensive private colleges. On the other hand, Rush was born in Georgia and grew up in Chicago's Southside. He attended Chicago's own Roosevelt University. This implied that Obama was privileged and out of touch with Chicago's African-American community.

Rush also blasted Obama's short time in politics. He claimed that Obama had not "been around the first congressional district long enough to really see what's going on."[8]

Bobby Rush answers questions during an interview on October 6, 2005. Obama ran against Rush in the 2000 race to be a member of the U.S. House of Representatives.

Obama's campaign had trouble raising money. According to Dan Shomon, they were able to raise five hundred thirty-five thousand dollars.[9] That seems like a lot, but advertising costs are very expensive. It was not enough money for Obama's campaign to advertise on television. Without television advertising, it was impossible for Obama's message to reach enough voters to make a difference.

Nothing seemed to go right. During Christmas week, Obama flew with his family to visit his grandmother in Hawaii. He was planning on returning in five days. However, eighteen-month-old Malia got sick in Hawaii. She was unable to fly. Obama would not leave his daughter behind, so he stayed with her.

In doing so, he missed an important state legislature vote about gun control. The city's biggest newspaper, *The Chicago Tribune*, wrote that Obama missed the vote because he "had decided to remain on vacation in Hawaii."[10] Although he was with his family tending to a sick baby, the article made it sound as if was frolicking on a beach.

On the plus side, Obama did well in some debates with Rush. He also received good coverage for his ideas about health care and education. But it was too little, too late. Obama was crushed in the primary election, losing to Rush by a two-to-one margin.[11]

Although Obama is an adult in the public eye, he is a human being with the same emotions as others. He admitted that he took his loss as a personal rejection by the people of Chicago. He said that no matter where he went in town, people saw him as a loser. He said he felt "the sorts of feelings that most people haven't experienced since high school, when the girl you'd been pining over dismissed you with a joke in front of her friends, or you missed a pair of free throws with the big game on the line—the kinds of feelings that most adults wisely organize their lives to avoid."[12]

Losing the election, and by such a wide margin, may have been depressing for Obama, but there was some joy in the family household not long afterwards. In 2001, Michelle gave birth to another daughter, Sasha.

Then came September 11, 2001. On that Tuesday morning, nineteen radical Arab Muslim terrorists hijacked four commercial airplanes in the United States. Two

Obama sits next to his wife, Michelle, and daughters Sasha
(far left) and Malia in 2004.

airplanes were flown into the two towers of New York's
World Trade Center office buildings. Another was flown
into the Pentagon building outside Washington, D.C.
The Pentagon is the headquarters of the United States
Department of Defense. The fourth airplane crashed in
rural Pennsylvania after passengers fought the hijackers.
It is believed that the airplane was being hijacked to
Washington, D.C., to crash into either the White House
or the United States Capitol.

Nearly three thousand innocent people died that day. The vast majority were in New York City. Obama heard about the first crash on his car radio while driving in Chicago to a meeting. At first he thought it was an accidental plane crash. By the time he arrived at his meeting, the second plane had crashed into the second World Trade Center tower. That made it clear it was no accident.

The terrorists were agents of Al Qaeda, a Muslim-based terrorist group founded in 1988 by a Saudi Arabian named Osama bin Laden. In 2001, Al Qaeda was headquartered in the mid-Asian nation of Afghanistan. President George W. Bush declared war on Al Qaeda, and the United States invaded Afghanistan. Nearly all of the United States Congress supported the President. The majority of nations across the world also supported the United States.

In 2002, President Bush began to publicly support an invasion of another Muslim nation: Iraq. Bush said Iraq was involved in the attacks on September 11, 2001. He also stated that Iraq had weapons of mass destruction. The majority of Americans believed Bush.

But not Obama.

On October 2, 2002, Obama spoke in Chicago to a rally of people opposed to going to war in Iraq. It was a bold move. Numerous conservatives accused those against the war of being un-American. Still, Obama took the risk of making a public speech there.

He addressed the crowd:

> Let me begin by saying that although this has been
> billed as an anti-war rally, I stand before you as some-
> one who is not opposed to war in all circumstances.
> The Civil War was one of the bloodiest in history,
> and yet it was only through the crucible of the sword,
> the sacrifice of multitudes, that we could begin to
> perfect this union, and drive the scourge of slavery
> from our soil.
>
> I don't oppose all wars. My grandfather signed up
> for a war the day after Pearl Harbor was bombed,
> fought in Patton's army. He saw the dead and dying
> across the fields of Europe; he heard the stories
> of fellow troops who first entered Auschwitz and
> Treblinka. He fought in the name of a larger
> freedom, part of that arsenal of democracy that tri-
> umphed over evil, and he did not fight in vain. I don't
> oppose all wars.
>
> After September 11th, after witnessing the
> carnage and destruction, the dust and the tears, I
> supported this administration's pledge to hunt down
> and root out those who would slaughter innocents in
> the name of intolerance, and I would willingly take
> up arms myself to prevent such tragedy from hap-
> pening again. I don't oppose all wars. And I know
> that in this crowd today, there is no shortage of patri-
> ots, or of patriotism.[13]

Obama stated that the Bush administration's war plans
with Iraq were a distraction from his political problems.
Obama announced he was against a war with Iraq since

it would be "a dumb war . . . a rash war . . . a war based not on reason but on passion, not on principle but on politics."[14]

His speech did not hurt his standing with his constituents. Obama ran unopposed for reelection in 2002. In that election, the Democrats won control of the Illinois State Senate. When the Illinois State Senate took control in January 2003, Obama was named chairman of the Senate's Health and Human Services Committee. That same month, Obama made a stunning announcement. He was going to run for the United States Senate in the November 2004 election.

On March 20, 2003, the United States invaded Iraq. War had begun.

> Obama announced he was against a war with Iraq since it would be "a dumb war . . . a rash war."

Chapter 9

"Are You Making Other People's Lives a Little Bit Better?"

Against the backdrop of war, Barack Obama began his campaign for a seat in the United States Senate. There were six other candidates running for the Democratic nomination, and Obama was one of the lesser known.

His toughest opponent was millionaire Blair Hull. Hull had spent $29 million on his campaign.[1] With that kind of money, he received exposure that long shots such as Obama could only dream of. So not surprisingly, Hull was the top-ranked candidate for most of the campaign.

It was natural that Obama had support in Chicago's Southside. However, some white communities surrounding

Chicago had histories of racial intolerance. Riots broke out in 1966 when Martin Luther King, Jr., brought what he planned as a nonviolent protest to some of these towns.

In addition, much of central and southern Illinois have more in common with the conservative southern states than northern Illinois. The city of Cairo in Illinois's southern tip is closer to Mississippi than to Chicago. Ku Klux Klan activity took place in Cairo as recently as the 1960s.

Sadly, there is still bigotry in the United States. But it is not as widespread as it was forty years earlier. When Obama spoke to the residents of southern Illinois, he won them over with jokes about people always mispronouncing his name. Then he stressed how despite different backgrounds, all Americans share the same values.

In the city of Decatur in central Illinois, two big factories had recently closed. As a result, thousands of residents lost jobs. When he campaigned in Decatur, Obama blasted the Bush administration as favoring the wealthy people over the less well off. He announced, "We have an administration that believes that the government's role is to protect the powerful from the powerless."[2] It was not long before people in southern and central Illinois were sporting "Obama for Senate" campaign buttons.

In the white suburbs of Chicago, Obama stressed again that he did not oppose all wars, only unwise wars. He also emphasized how he refused to resort to dirty politics. Voters were won over by his gift as a speaker. One young Democrat official, Ryan Marucco, said, "I just never heard anybody speak like him before. It's like he's talking to you, and not a crowd."[3]

Meanwhile, his opponents' campaigns faltered. Hull lost popularity due to a personal scandal. He admitted that he had physically hurt his ex-wife.[4]

Obama's campaign raised enough money to blitz the state with television ads just prior to the primary election. His ability to reach all voters, plus the failures of his main opponents, helped Obama win the primary election with 53 percent of the vote.[5]

Now that he was the Democratic nominee, he had to face the Republican nominee in the general election for the Senate seat. Obama's opponent was Jack Ryan, a strong conservative with movie-star good looks. Indeed, his ex-wife was Jeri Ryan, a former beauty pageant contestant and actress. She had costarred on television programs *Star Trek: Voyager* and *Boston Public*. But as had happened with Blair Hull, the media discovered negative personal details about the Ryans' marriage. Under pressure, Ryan dropped out of the race in August.

With the election in November, Republicans rushed to find a replacement candidate. They chose another African American, Alan Keyes.

Keyes has always had a reputation as a loose cannon, someone who makes outrageous statements. That proved

Alan Keyes, Obama's Competitor

Although the overwhelming majority of African Americans are Democrats, Keyes is a strong conservative. Many see Keyes as an extreme conservative. Like Obama, Keyes is a highly intelligent man, with degrees from Cornell University and Harvard University.

Keyes had much going against him during the race for the U.S. Senate seat. He was a longtime resident of Maryland, not Illinois. Keyes moved to Illinois just to run in the Senate race. That made many Illinois residents wonder if he had the best interests of Illinois citizens at heart.

Obama and Republican Alan Keyes square off on October 26, 2004, in Chicago during the final debate in the race for the open U.S. Senate seat from Illinois.

true when he said, "Christ would not vote for Barack Obama because Barack Obama has voted to behave in a way that it is inconceivable for Christ to have behaved."[6]

Reaction against that comment brought widespread condemnation. Obama responded, as he often does, with a joke. He said at least Keyes did not call him the Antichrist.

It did not matter. Keyes never had a real chance. In the election, Obama received 70 percent of the vote. Keyes had only 27 percent.[7] Obama took the oath of office as United States senator from Illinois on January 4, 2005.

A few months later, Obama introduced his first bill. It would have increased financial aid to needy college students. Obama toured colleges and universities throughout Illinois in hopes of bringing attention to his bill. President Bush agreed that aid for college students should be increased. But he did not want to increase it as much as Obama did. With Republicans in control of the Senate, Obama's bill died in committee and was never voted on by the Senate.

The experience was troubling. After eight years in the Illinois State Senate, Obama's name was well recognized in his state and he wielded some clout. But in the United States Senate, he was almost unknown. He quickly learned the ways of big-time politics and was disappointed.

Obama said of Washington politics, "It can be incredibly frustrating. The maneuverings, the chicanery, the smallness of politics here."[8]

Barack Obama and his wife and daughters are covered in confetti after Obama delivered his acceptance speech in Chicago on November 2, 2004. Earlier that evening, he was elected U.S. senator from Illinois.

Once, when listening to a senator give a long-winded speech, Obama reacted like a student would to a boring teacher. He handed a three-word note to a staff member. It read simply, "Shoot. Me. Now."[9]

It became clear that to get anything accomplished, Obama would have to cooperate with members of the Republican majority. So he did just that.

In May 2005, Obama cosponsored a bill with Arizona Republican Senator John McCain. It was titled the "Secure America and Orderly Immigration Act." Its purpose was to help control illegal immigration to the United States. The bill was passed by the Senate, but not the House of Representatives. However, Obama was not finished with the idea.

In the meantime, he was busy with other projects. Part of a senator's duties include fact-finding missions, or research trips, in order to make better laws. In August 2005, he traveled with Indiana Republican Senator Richard Lugar to Russia, Ukraine, and Azerbaijan. All three were once part of the superpower the Union of Soviet Socialist Republics (USSR) before it crumbled in 1991. The trip's purpose was to find ways to reduce the world's weapons supply.

Obama took a second trip in January 2006. The destination was the Middle East. There he spoke with a group of Palestinian students in the Palestinian territories. The Palestinians were about to elect members of Hamas, a militant political party, as their leaders. One Hamas goal is to destroy Israel. Obama told the students that the United States will not recognize Hamas until it accepts Israel's right to exist. He said any Palestinian government must be able to "negotiate as a reliable partner with Israel."[10]

In August 2006, Obama went on a fact-finding mission to Kenya with Michelle and their two daughters. Over ten thousand Kenyans cheered him as he rode through the streets in a truck. Obama said, "I just want to say very quickly that I am so proud to come back home. It means a lot to me that the people of my father, my grandfather, are here in such huge crowds."[11]

In a speech at the University of Nairobi that was televised across the nation, Obama condemned corruption in Kenyan politics. That drew mixed reactions. Some Kenyans welcomed his remarks while others thought Kenya's politics were none of his business.

He and Michelle also took voluntary tests for the HIV virus, which causes AIDS. Over a million of Kenya's 32 million people are infected with the HIV virus.[12] Obama announced, "I and my wife are personally taking HIV tests. And if someone all the way from America can come and do that, then you have no excuse."[13]

> Obama announced, "I and my wife are personally taking HIV tests."

The Obamas took the time to visit relatives, including Auma and Obama's grandmother. He also visited the graves of his father and grandfather.

The next month Obama was back in Washington. On September 26, President Bush signed a bill sponsored by Obama and Oklahoma Republican Senator Tom Coburn. Coburn was regarded as one of the most conservative United States senators. Yet even though he and Obama see most issues differently, the Democrat and Republican agreed on one thing: taxpayers have a right to know how their money is spent.

The two senators sponsored the Coburn-Obama Transparency Act. It requires the federal government to create a Web site allowing citizens to track who receives federal funds.

Coburn and Obama released a statement at the time that read in part: "This legislation marks a small but important step in the effort to change the culture in Washington, D.C. American taxpayers soon will be equipped with a significant tool that will make it much easier to hold elected officials accountable for the way taxpayer money is spent."[14]

For all his charm, Obama is not above making enemies. In fall 2006 he voted for another version of the "Secure America and Orderly Immigration Act." This was called the "Secure Fence Act." It called for the construction of a seven hundred-mile-long fence along the United States-Mexico border. Its purpose is to try to stop immigrants crossing illegally from Mexico into the United States. Many Latino activists slammed Obama. They saw the Secure Fence Act as a sign of prejudice against Mexicans.

Many of Obama's actions had an antiwar and antimilitary message. Based on the trip Obama and Senator Richard Lugar took to the former USSR nations in 2005, the two senators sponsored a new bill making it easier to destroy weapons of mass destruction. President Bush signed it into law on January 11, 2007.

Then, on January 30 and February 7, 2007, Obama introduced two bills that would make it mandatory to

On October 17, 2006, Obama signed copies of a book he wrote called
The Audacity of Hope: Thoughts on Reclaiming the American Dream. The book's
main title came from a sermon he had heard at his church in Chicago.

bring American troops home from the Iraq war. Obama
stated, "Our troops have performed brilliantly in Iraq, but
no amount of American soldiers can solve the political
differences at the heart of somebody else's civil war."[15]

Being a senator means spending a lot of time away
from family. Obama likes to make the most of the time
he spends with his. For one of his daughter's birthdays he

went out of his way to order pizza and balloons for her party.

Yet like most parents, he can be embarrassing to his kids. When eight-year-old Malia introduced her father to one of her friends, he bent over to shake the friend's hand. Malia scolded her dad, saying kids today don't shake hands. She claimed, "This is the 21st Century, Dad. . . . Maybe they say 'hey.' They might wave. But they do not shake hands."

Obama apologized, "I'm sorry to embarrass you."

Malia responded, "That's okay, Daddy. You didn't know any better."[16]

On February 10, 2007, Obama made a special trip to the Illinois capital of Springfield, where he had worked for eight years as a state senator. It was a freezing cold day, but about fifteen thousand fans stood outdoors to hear Obama speak.[17] Standing in front of the Old State Capitol where Abraham Lincoln once served, Obama declared his candidacy for the Democratic nomination for president of the United States.

Obama announced:

> As Lincoln organized the forces arrayed against slavery, he was heard to say: "Of strange, discordant, and even hostile elements, we gathered from the four winds, and formed and fought to battle through." That is our purpose here today. That's why I'm in this race. Not just to hold an office, but to gather

with you to transform a nation. I want to win that next battle—for justice and opportunity.[18]

Being a presidential candidate means much scrutiny. All sorts of questions about Obama were being asked. Many wondered if a person with only two years in the Senate is experienced enough to be president.

In response, Obama supporters point to his life experience. That includes his years as a community organizer,

Senator Obama arrives to announce his candidacy
for president of the United States outside the Old State Capitol
in Springfield, Illinois, on February 10, 2007.

his work in voter registration, his time teaching law, and his unusual background. Kirk Dillard says, "He has lived abroad and has relatives who are certainly not your Mayflower Americans and understands different cultures. Many presidents with foreign-policy experience have not lived firsthand the type of life that Barack has."[19]

Others stress that Abraham Lincoln's experience in the Senate was just as brief as Obama's.

Race is another issue. Every American president has been a white, male Christian. Only one, John F. Kennedy, was not a Protestant. Obama insists the United States is ready for an African-American president. He says, " . . . what I've found is that the American people—once they get to know you—are going to judge you on your individual character."[20]

Obama has to deal with race questions from African Americans as well as whites. Because he is not a descendant of slaves, some African Americans say that he does not represent them. They think his background is more similar to the immigrant experience.

African-American author Deborah Dickerson answered the question "Is Barack Obama black?" by saying, "No he's not, in the American political context, black means the descendent of West African slaves brought here to labor in the United States. It's not a put-down, not to say he hasn't suffered. It's not to say that he doesn't have a glorious lineage of his own. It's just to say, that he and I, who am descended from West African slaves brought to America. We are not the same."[21]

Obama said publicly that he does not believe African Americans should vote for him because of his skin color. He stated, "A black candidate has to earn black votes the same way he's gotta earn white votes. And that's exactly how it should be."[22]

Conservative Republicans have dug into Obama's past to try and find something negative about him. That strategy is referred to as smear tactics. Unfortunately, it is common in much of politics. Americans say they dislike smear tactics, but they take place just the same.

Even before Obama declared he was running for president, a conservative magazine titled *Insight* published an article stating that Obama attended a radical Islamic school in Indonesia. This was repeated on the conservative Fox News network. Since radical Muslims were responsible for the events of September 11, 2001, that was a very serious charge. It also turned out to be totally false.[23]

One negative story about Obama's past was true. It was learned in January 2007 that he had never paid fifteen parking tickets he received while attending Harvard Law School nearly twenty years earlier. Obama went ahead and paid them, including late fees.

In August 2007, Obama stated that although he is against the Iraq War, he is devoted to fighting terror and bringing those guilty of the September 11 attacks to

Obama stated that although he is against the Iraq War, he is devoted to fighting terror.

justice. It is widely believed that many members of Al-Qaeda are hiding in Pakistan. In a speech he gave on August 1, 2007, Obama said that he is willing to use military force against Al-Qaeda in Pakistan even without Pakistan's permission.

He stressed, "The first step must be getting off the wrong battlefield in Iraq and taking the fight to the terrorists in Afghanistan and Pakistan."[24]

Since declaring himself a candidate for president, Obama has sworn that he will quit his habit of smoking cigarettes. He is concerned about his health. But he also wishes to set a good example.

Values are a concern of Obama. He said to talk show host Oprah Winfrey, "You know, we reward people a lot for being rich or being famous or being cute or being thin . . . one of the values that I think we need to instill in our country, in our children, is a sense, are you useful? Are you useful to other people? . . . Are you making other people's lives a little bit better?"[25]

Chapter 10

Change Comes to America

R unning for president of the United States is a long, grueling process. First, the candidate has to win the nomination of his or her party. To be nominated, candidates enter a series of political contests. There is one held in every state. The more votes they get in each, the more delegates are pledged to vote for them. The Democratic party also has "super delegates." These are party leaders and elected officials who can vote for whichever candidate they choose. When one candidate receives a certain amount of delegates, he or she has unofficially received the nomination. For the Democratic party, the total is 2,118. The official nominating process takes place at a major party convention the summer before the general election.

Along with Obama, there were eight additional Democrats trying to earn their party's nomination.

Democratic Presidential hopefuls Joe Biden, Bill Richardson, Dennis Kucinich, Hillary Rodham Clinton, Barack Obama, Christopher Dodd, and John Edwards (left to right) share the stage prior to a debate at the University of Las Vegas, Nevada, on November 15, 2007.

There were three other sitting senators: Joe Biden from Delaware, Christopher Dodd from Connecticut, and Hillary Rodham Clinton from New York. Clinton is a former first lady and is married to former president Bill Clinton. There was one sitting governor, Bill Richardson from New Mexico; and one sitting member of the House of Representatives, Dennis Kucinich from Ohio. Rounding out the group were two former senators: John Edwards from North Carolina and Mike Gravel from Alaska; and one former governor, Tom Vilsack from Iowa.

Although these candidates were competing with each other, they all had one thing in common. Each was a strong critic of sitting President Bush and the Iraq War. At the first debate among the Democratic candidates, Obama made an emotional statement about the war: "When I listen to mothers and fathers all across America, they are telling me it's time to come home."[1]

The candidates spent 2007 campaigning throughout the country. However, they spent most of their time in two states: Iowa and New Hampshire, the sites of the first two presidential contests. Most eyes were on Clinton. As the person with the most recognizable name, she was thought by many to be the favorite for the nomination.

The first presidential contest is the Iowa Caucus. It took place on January 3, 2008. A caucus is a meeting where active members of each party gather. At the meeting, each must openly declare who they support for their party's nomination. Obama won the Iowa Caucus with ease, taking 38 percent of the votes. John Edwards came in second, with 30 percent. Hillary Rodham Clinton finished in a disappointing third place, with 29 percent.[2]

Political analysts said that the Iowa caucus could be the beginning of the end for Clinton. However, many also said that Iowa Caucus results can be misleading. Since people attending the caucus must verbally say who they support, the caucus tends mostly to draw political activists, or those who take an active interest in politics. People who are not avidly interested in politics tend not to attend the caucuses.

The New Hampshire Primary took place on January 8. Unlike the Iowa Caucus, New Hampshire holds a traditional election with secret ballots. Political polls taken shortly before the election showed Obama ahead of Clinton by nine percent.[3] Yet, New Hampshire voters can be quirky, and often change their minds. Those who predicted doom for Clinton were in for a surprise. Clinton beat Obama, winning 39 percent of the vote to Obama's 37 percent.[4]

Although Clinton won by just two points, her victory was a major upset. The New Hampshire primary gave her campaign new life. Obama was gracious in defeat, but said he would continue to fight on. Yet over the next few weeks, Clinton won primary elections in Michigan and Florida as well as the Nevada caucus. Obama won only the South Carolina primary.

On February 5, a total of twenty-two states held Democratic party caucuses or primary elections. That date became known as Super Tuesday. If either Obama or Clinton won a clear majority of states, he or she would have a huge lead that would be hard to overtake. Yet after all the votes were counted on Super Tuesday, Obama had won thirteen states and Clinton had won nine. Obama had a slight edge in delegates, but hardly a commanding lead.

By then it was clear that this would be a two-person race between Obama and Clinton. The other candidates gradually dropped out. By early March Arizona Senator John McCain had sewn up the Republican nomination for president. He was a seventy-one-year-old Vietnam War hero who had spent years as a prisoner of war in North Vietnam. If he won the general election, he would be the oldest person ever elected president.

Obama addresses his supporters at a New Hampshire rally on January 8, 2008.

As the campaign season went on, the Democratic race started to take on a negative tone. Clinton accused Obama of not having enough experience to be president. Meanwhile, Obama stepped up criticism of Clinton. He criticized her for originally voting to approve the war in Iraq.

Then on March 13, a bombshell was dropped. ABC News had been researching sermons given by Obama's minister, Jeremiah Wright. The staff discovered that Wright had made many comments that appeared to be anti-American. The one that bothered people most was a comment one would hardly expect a minister to say.

In a 2003 sermon, Wright told his congregation that America has not treated African Americans fairly. He then added, "The government gives them the drugs, builds bigger prisons, passes a three-strike law and then wants us to sing, 'God Bless America.' No, no, no, God damn America, that's in the Bible for killing innocent people."[5]

Many Americans found it disturbing that Obama would attend such a church. Obama stated that he disapproved of those remarks by Wright. But he also said he agreed with some of Wright's views on social issues. That hardly settled the controversy. Wright's words were becoming a distraction to Obama's campaign. Obama could have ignored the Wright issue or tried to sidestep it somehow. Instead, Obama took an unusual course for a politician: He decided to face the issue, directly and honestly. "I want to do a speech on race," he told his top adviser, David Axelrod.[6] Obama would spend three nights working on the speech, which he delivered at Philadelphia's Constitution Hall on March 19:

> Given my background, my politics, and my professed values and ideals, there will no doubt be those for whom my statements of condemnation [of Reverend Wright] are not enough. Why associate myself with Reverend Wright in the first place, they may ask? Why not join another church? And I confess that if all that I knew of Reverend Wright were the snippets of those sermons that have run in an endless loop on the television and You Tube, or if Trinity United

Church of Christ conformed to the caricatures being peddled by some commentators, there is no doubt that I would react in much the same way.[7]

. . . But the truth is, that isn't all that I know of the man. The man I met more than twenty years ago is a man who helped introduce me to my Christian faith, a man who spoke to me about our obligations to love one another; to care for the sick and lift up the poor. He is a man who served his country as a U.S. Marine; who has studied and lectured at some of the finest universities and seminaries in the country, and who for over thirty years led a church that serves the community by doing God's work here on Earth—by housing the homeless, ministering to the needy, providing day care services and scholarships and prison ministries, and reaching out to those suffering from HIV/AIDS.[8]

Perhaps the most memorable part of the speech was Obama's personal statement about his grandmother: "I can no more disown him [Wright] than I can my white grandmother—a woman who helped raise me, a woman who sacrificed again and again for me, a woman who loves me as much as she loves anything in this world, but a woman who once confessed her fear of black men who passed by her on the street, and who on more than one occasion has uttered racial or ethnic stereotypes that made me cringe.

"These people are a part of me. And they are a part of America, this country that I love."[9]

Backstage, after Obama was finished with the speech, many of his aides and friends, as well as his wife, Michelle, were in tears.[10] Obama later stated, "My gut was telling me that this was a teachable moment, and that if I tried to do the usual damage control instead of talking to the American people like they were adults and could understand the complexities of race, I would be not only doing damage to the campaign but missing an opportunity for leadership."[11]

Unfortunately, the Wright issue did not end with Obama's moving speech. Wright would go on to make appearances on several television shows and continued to make controversial statements. During an interview with Bill Moyers, he also said that Obama "goes out as a politician and says what he has to say as a politician. I continue to be a pastor who speaks to the people of God about the things of God."[12]

Obama reacted with anger and dismay. During a press conference the following day, April 29, he responded:

> I am outraged by the comments that were made and saddened by the spectacle that we saw yesterday. . . The person that I saw yesterday [Wright] was not the person that I met twenty years ago. His comments were not only divisive and destructive, but I believe that they end up giving comfort to those who prey on hate, and I believe that they do not portray accurately the perspective of the black church. They certainly don't portray accurately my values and beliefs. And if

Reverend Wright thinks that that's political posturing, as he put it, then he doesn't know me very well. And based on his remarks yesterday, well, I may not know him as well as I thought either.[13]

Almost immediately afterward, the Obamas resigned their membership in Wright's church.

Meanwhile, throughout the spring, several more caucuses and primary elections took place. Clinton and Obama each won several contests, but neither won enough to take the nomination. At this point there was some concern that the "super delegates" might decide the process and possibly ignore the will of the majority of voters. But as time went on, the majority of these delegates pledged their support to Obama—fairly reflecting the momentum Obama had earned with the pledged delegates.

The last day of primary elections was June 3. When Obama won the Montana primary that day, he earned enough delegates to top the magic number of 2,118. Obama was the Democratic party nominee for president. Obama chose as his running mate a former opponent, Senator Joe Biden of Delaware. Biden has much foreign policy experience which would be a great resource for Obama if he was elected.

The Democratic National Convention took place in Denver, Colorado, from August 25 through August 28. On August 28, Obama gave his acceptance speech in the football stadium where the Denver Broncos play home games. A record thirty-eight million people watched it on television.[14]

In his speech, Obama did his best to link McCain with the unpopular President Bush. He said, "the record's clear: John McCain has voted with George Bush 90 percent of the time. Senator McCain likes to talk about judgment, but, really, what does it say about your judgment when you think George Bush has been right more than 90 percent of the time?"[15]

Obama stressed that the government should take part in making Americans' lives better. He stated:

> Our government should work for us, not against us. It should help us, not hurt us. It should ensure opportunity not just for those with the most money and influence, but for every American who's willing to work. That's the promise of America, the idea that we are responsible for ourselves, but that we also rise or fall as one nation, the fundamental belief that I am my brother's keeper, I am my sister's keeper. That's the promise we need to keep. That's the change we need right now.[16]

Obama went on to spell out the changes he feels America needs. He promised to invest in clean energy sources to reduce the United States's dependence on foreign oil. He promised to cut taxes for working families and stop giving tax break to companies that hire very low paid workers in other countries rather than American workers. He promised to pay teachers better, but at the same time demand better job performances. He promised affordable health care for every American. Furthermore, he promised to quickly end the war in Iraq while stepping up the search to find Osama bin-Laden.

The Republican convention followed a week later. It was held in St. Paul, Minnesota. McCain's choice of a running mate was much more surprising than Obama's. He chose Governor Sarah Palin of Alaska.

McCain played himself up as a maverick politician. That meant that he did not support his fellow Republicans on every issue. Instead, he supported what he felt was right, even if he angered his fellow Republicans in doing so. Palin was known in Alaska as a maverick politician as well.

As soon as the conventions were over, the four candidates—Obama, Biden, McCain, and Palin—began campaigning across the United States. Each flew from city to city to give speeches and meet voters. Obama continued to link McCain to Bush. McCain said that Obama's policies were too liberal for the nation. McCain also criticized Obama as being too inexperienced for the job as president. And while Obama did not bring up McCain's age, others did. They suggested that a person in his seventies might not be in condition for the demanding job of president.

In order for the voters to get to know the candidates better, a series of debates was scheduled. There would be three between Obama and McCain and one between Biden and Palin.

While the candidates were campaigning, other events that would influence voters took place. Banks and other businesses that lend money to people had made foolish decisions. Many lent money to people who could not afford to pay it back. As a result, these banks and other lending businesses were failing. The economy was so weak that it was being said that the United States was in a recession. A recession is a very poor economic situation which usually includes a decline in people's incomes, a large unemployment rate and a low growth rate in the nation's general overall economic condition.

Experts have debated how much Bush's policies had to do with this. But the fact is that this problem happened while Bush was in his eighth year as president. Since McCain had voted in agreement so often with Bush's policies, Americans could not help but connect McCain and Bush. Obama and his supporters would not let the voters forget it.

The first two presidential debates were very matter-of-fact. There were no major announcements or mistakes by either candidate. The same held true for the one vice-presidential debate. But as the nation's economic news was getting worse and worse, McCain and Palin were getting desperate. They began to attack Obama personally.

Obama debates Republican candidate John McCain at Hofstra University in Hempstead, New York, on October 15, 2008.

One of the nastiest attacks had to do with a man named Bill Ayers. Today Ayers is an education professor at the University of Illinois at Chicago. But in the 1960s he co-founded a left-wing, radical student organization called the Weather Underground. Part of the Weather Underground's tactics included setting off bombs at public buildings and monuments with the purpose of destroying them. The group never targeted people, however. Also, Ayers had long given up these violent tactics.

Obama and Ayers had met a few times in their careers, but they never had a close working relationship.[17] Still, McCain and Plain publicly linked Obama with Ayers and played up Ayers's violent past. In one interview, McCain asked how anyone could support "someone who was engaged in bombings that could have or did kill innocent people?"[18] At a fund-raising event, Sarah Palin went so far as to say, "Our opponent [Obama] though, is someone who sees America, it seems, as being so imperfect that he's palling around with terrorists who would target their own country."[19]

Obama supporters were outraged that the Republicans would exaggerate Obama's limited connections with Ayers. And when McCain brought William Ayers up in the third debate, Obama was ready with an answer:

> Mr. Ayers has become the centerpiece of Senator McCain's campaign over the last two or three weeks. This has been their primary focus. So let's get the record straight. Bill Ayers is a professor of education in Chicago. Forty years ago, when I was eight years old, he engaged in despicable acts with a radical domestic group. I have roundly condemned those acts. Ten years ago he served and I served on a school reform board that was funded by one of Ronald Reagan's former ambassadors and close friends, Mr. Annenberg.
>
> Other members on that board were the presidents of the University of Illinois, the president of Northwestern University, who happens to be a Republican, the president of *The Chicago Tribune*, a Republican-leaning newspaper. Mr. Ayers is not involved in my campaign. He has never been

involved in this campaign. And he will not advise me in the White House. So that's Mr. Ayers.[20]

McCain continued to try to link Obama with Ayers. However, it did not work. With the war in Iraq dragging on and the economy in rough shape, Americans were hungry for change. But on what should have been the eve of the happiest moment in Obama's life, some tears were shed by the Obama family. On the morning of November 3, the day before the election, Obama's grandmother—the woman he called Toot—died.

Obama and his sister Maya released a statement to the media. It read in part, "It is with great sadness that we announce that our grandmother, Madelyn Dunham, has died peacefully after a battle with cancer. She was the cornerstone of our family, and a woman of extraordinary accomplishment, strength, and humility."[21] At a political rally in Charlotte, North Carolina, Obama told the gathered crowd that his grandmother was, "one of those quiet heroes, we have across America, who aren't famous . . . but each and every day they work hard. They look after their families. They look after their children and their grandchildren."[22]

Before she died, however, Obama's grandmother did vote for her grandson. Hawaii is one of several states that allows its citizens to vote early.

On November 4, Obama was overwhelmingly elected president. He and Biden received fifty-two percent of the vote compared to McCain and Palin's forty-six percent.[23] More importantly, Obama and Biden received 364 electoral votes while McCain and Palin received 174.[24] Obama even won states that had not voted for a Democrat for president in years. These included Virginia, North Carolina, and Indiana.

At about 11:00 P.M. eastern standard time, Obama delivered a victory speech before a huge throng of supporters in Chicago's Grant Park. Celebrities and political

President-Elect Barack Obama greets the crowd at Chicago's Grant Park just prior to delivering his acceptance speech on election night, November 4, 2008.

figures mingled with everyday people in the crowd. Jesse Jackson and Oprah Winfrey wept uncontrollably. Obama told them all:

> If there is anyone out there who still doubts that America is a place where all things are possible, who still wonders if the dream of our founders is alive in our time, who still questions the power of our democracy, tonight is your answer. . . . It's been a long time coming, but tonight, because of what we did on this day, in this election, at this defining moment, change has come to America.
>
> . . . America, we have come so far. We have seen so much. But there is so much more to do. So tonight, let us ask ourselves: if our children should live to see the next century, what change will they see? What progress will we have made?
>
> This is our chance to answer that call. This is our moment. This is our time.[25]

Political analysts had different explanations as to why Obama won so convincingly. Some said voters felt McCain would continue the failed policies of President Bush. Others praised Obama for running a very well-organized, high-tech, and well-run campaign. Still others credited him for rallying young voters.

Political pollster Peter D. Hart said, "[Al] Gore [the Democratic nominee in 2000] carried young voters by two points. [John] Kerry carried them by about nine points. Obama carried them by 34 points."[26]

Chapter 11

"The Journey We Continue Today"

T he election of any United States president makes headlines across the world. But the election of Obama was even more noteworthy. People everywhere bought newspapers the morning of November 5 to save for future generations. Many newspaper headlines referred to Obama breaking a racial barrier. The headline of *The Star-Ledger* (of Newark, New Jersey) read, "Obama Reaches The Mountaintop."[1] This was a reference to a line from the legendary speech given by Dr. Martin Luther King over forty years earlier.

The national newspaper *USA Today*, blared in bold letters, "A Dream Fulfilled."[2] *USA Today* reporter Rick Hampson wrote, "The day was a long time coming, and when Wednesday finally dawned, a lot of bleary-eyed, partied-out Americans had to pinch themselves: They had an African-American president-elect."[3] Even newspapers in the Deep South—a hotbed of legal segregation less than fifty years prior—celebrated the breaking of the racial barrier. On *The Anniston Star* in Alabama, the head-line read, "In Our Lifetime."[4]

The historic excitement of this American election was felt overseas, too. The headline of *The London Times* was, "American voters honour [sic] Martin Luther King's Dream with Victory for Obama."[5] Wild celebrations broke out from Kenya, the homeland of Obama's father, to Indonesia, where Obama once attended school.

Reporters talked to veterans of the civil rights move-ment. Taylor Rogers, an eighty-two-year-old man, had been a sanitation worker in Memphis, Tennessee. He attended that legendary speech Martin Luther King gave there the night before he was assassinated. Rogers said to Rick Hampson, "This was Dr. King's dream—to have someone in the black community to represent us, and bring the races together."[6]

Obama would not be sworn in as president until January 20, 2009. Before that he had to choose his staff and cabinet. The day after the election, he picked Illinois congressman Rahm Emanuel to be his chief of staff. The chief of staff is the top aide to the president. His or her tasks include supervising the rest of the White House staff

Top: President-Elect Obama's half-brother Malik is carried by a jubilant crowd in Kogelo, Kenya, in the wake of the presidential election. Bottom: Young students at Obama's former school in Jakarta, Indonesia, also celebrated Obama's election.

and trying to get the president's agenda approved by Congress and the American people. With those responsibilities, the chief of staff has to be an aggressive person. Emanuel has always been known as a man who hates to take no for an answer.

As the month of November went on, Obama selected more staff and cabinet members. The cabinet is made up of the top officers of the executive branch of the government. These officers are usually referred to by the title of secretary. George Washington had four cabinet members: the secretary of state, or the person in charge of the nation's foreign affairs; the secretary of the treasury; the secretary of war; and the attorney general. Today there are fifteen cabinet positions.

Obama had said while he was campaigning that, as president, he would select for his cabinet a "team of rivals."[7] He took this phrase from the title of a best-selling book about President Lincoln. Lincoln chose former political opponents to be in his cabinet. Obama decided to follow Lincoln's example by working with political opponents to do what is best for the nation. Obama promised that he would have at least one Republican in his cabinet.[8]

Obama kept that promise. He announced that he was keeping President Bush's secretary of defense, Robert Gates. With wars raging in Afghanistan and Iraq, Obama wanted to keep Gates because of his experience and knowledge.[9]

Obama also selected for the cabinet three of his former rivals for the Democratic presidential nomination. Former Iowa governor Tom Vilsack was chosen to be secretary of agriculture. New Mexico Governor Bill Richardson was picked to be secretary of commerce. One choice that surprised many was Hillary Clinton for the important post of secretary of state.

After Obama finished making his staff selections, there was one more choice to make. For a long time, his daughters Malia and Sasha wanted a dog. Obama said if he was elected president he would buy them one. People from all over wrote to him to suggest their favorite breeds. Obama joked, "We're getting more advice about this than my economic policies."[10]

The dog question became a lighthearted distraction during a tough time. At a press conference just days after the election, Obama told reporters: "We have two criteria that have to be reconciled. One is that Malia is allergic, so it [the dog] has to be hypoallergenic. There are a number of breeds that are hypoallergenic. On the other hand, our preference would be to get a shelter dog, but, obviously, a lot of shelter dogs are mutts like me. So whether we're going to be able to balance those two things I think is a pressing issue on the Obama household."[11]

To take a break from politics, Obama took his family on a vacation in late December to his native state, Hawaii. The president-elect took some time to play basketball with old high school friends, and go to the beach. One day, he took his family and some friends to Sea Life Park, a marine amusement park, and then went to a shopping mall.

Onlookers constantly snapped photographs of the Obamas. The media followed him constantly, reporting every detail of the trip. The respected newspaper, *The Washington Post*, even reported on what the Obamas ate for lunch. The president-elect had a tuna melt with tomatoes on twelve-grain bread, and a green and orange shaved ice for dessert. This was the public lifestyle the Obamas would have to get used to.

After returning from Hawaii, the Obamas moved to a temporary home in Washington. Obama's daughter Malia was looking forward to their move to the White House on January 20. She told her parents she would write school papers on President Lincoln's desk "because it will inspire big thoughts."[12]

The new year, 2009, had barely begun when Obama had to deal with another distraction. His choice for secretary of commerce, Bill Richardson, was in political trouble. He was suspected of giving government jobs to businesses mainly because they contributed to his presidential campaign. Richardson had not been convicted of anything, but because of the charges he felt he should withdraw his name as future secretary of commerce. He said, "I could not in good conscience ask the President-elect and his Administration to delay for one day the important work that needs to be done."[13] Obama regretfully accepted Richardson's resignation.

On January 7, Obama called for an unusual meeting at the White House. He invited the four living presidents together to advise him on what he could expect as president. It had been over twenty-seven years since the last group of all the living presidents had gathered in the same place.[14] A remarkable photograph of George H.W. Bush, Obama, George W. Bush, Bill Clinton and Jimmy Carter standing side by side in the White House was seen by people all over the world.

Obama said, "This is an extraordinary gathering. All the gentlemen here understand both the pressures and possibilities of the office. And for me to have the opportunity to get advice, good counsel and fellowship with these individuals is extraordinary. And I'm very grateful to all of them."[15]

Although Obama had blasted sitting President Bush during the campaign, Bush was very grateful to Obama at the meeting. Bush said, "All of us who have served in this office understand that the office transcends the individual. And we wish you all the very best. And so does the country."[16]

The next day, Obama gave a public speech outlining his plans to revive the sick economy. Such a move was highly unusual for a president-elect, but Obama felt the nation was so anxious about the economy that it was ready to hear his ideas.[17] They were a rejection of the Reagan-style policies of smaller government and tax breaks for the

George H. W. Bush, Barack Obama, George W. Bush, Bill Clinton, and Jimmy Carter, are photographed together in the Oval Office of the White House after their historic meeting on January 7, 2009.

wealthiest Americans. Although conservatives still basically believe in Reagan's economic theories, it was clear that many Americans felt those policies had led to the sad economic state the nation was in.[18]

Obama's plan includes giving tax cuts to middle income workers instead of the wealthy. He hoped to save or create three million jobs over the next few years.[19] He stressed that many of the new jobs will be in fields such as energy, education, and health care. Another part of Obama's recovery plan was to tighten laws so banks could no longer legally make foolish lending decisions.

There was so much excitement over the upcoming inauguration that Obama was featured in a January issue of the comic book series, *The Amazing Spider-Man*. In this issue, Spider-Man stops plans by the villain Chameleon to spoil Obama's inauguration. Obama had mentioned during the campaign that he enjoyed reading comics as a child. He said his favorite characters were Spider-Man and Conan the Barbarian. Joe Quesada is the editor in chief of Marvel Comics, which publishes the *Spider-Man* series. Quesada said, "It was a natural after we learned the new president is a Spider-Man fan. We thought, 'Fantastic! We have a comic-book geek in the White House.'"[20]

The idea of an African-American president was not welcome news to some Americans. White supremacist organizations, or groups who believe African-Americans and other people are inferior to white, European Christians, made threats to kill Obama. One such threat involving two white men from Arkansas and Tennessee was discovered and broken up. In New York City, three young men was arrested and charged with beating African Americans in retaliation for Obama's victory.[21]

Obama shook off the question of fears about his safety. He said, "I've got this pretty terrific crew of Secret Service guys that follow me wherever I go," and "I have a deep religious faith and a faith in people that carries me through the day."[22]

A few days before the inauguration, Obama wrote an open letter to his daughters. It appeared in *Parade* magazine. He wrote in part:

> Dear Malia and Sasha,
>
> I know that you've both had a lot of fun these last two years on the campaign trail, going to picnics and parades and state fairs, eating all sorts of junk food your mother and I probably shouldn't have let you have. But I also know that it hasn't always been easy for you and Mom, and that as excited as you both are about that new puppy, it doesn't make up for all the time we've been apart. I know how much I've missed these past two years, and today I want to tell you a little more about why I decided to take our family on this journey. . . .
>
> These are the things I want for you—to grow up in a world with no limits on your dreams and no achievements beyond your reach, and to grow into compassionate, committed women who will help build that world. And I want every child to have the same chances to learn and dream and grow and thrive that you girls have. That's why I've taken our family on this great adventure.
>
> I am so proud of both of you. I love you more than you can ever know. And I am grateful every day for your patience, poise, grace, and humor as we prepare to start our new life together in the White House.
>
> Love,
>
> Dad[23]

On Saturday, January 17, Barack Obama boarded a blue railroad car in Philadelphia. It was the beginning of a one hundred and thirty-seven mile train trip to Washington, D.C. He was retracing a part of the train trip Abraham Lincoln made in the winter of 1861 before his inauguration. Obama was also going to take the oath of office using the same Bible Lincoln used at his inauguration. Obama would be the first president to use the bible for his swearing in since Lincoln himself 148 years earlier.

Barack Obama and Joe Biden wave to the crowd in Edgewood, Maryland, during their inaugural whistle-stop train ride on Saturday, January 17, 2009.

Just before his train left Philadelphia, Obama referred to the city's history as he said, "We need a new declaration of independence—independence from ideology and small mindedness. . . . With this election, you provided once more that people who love this country can change it."[24] People in southeastern Pennsylvania, Delaware, and Maryland gathered along the tracks and waved as the train rolled by. Obama also spoke to well wishers at a few stops along the way. He arrived in Washington, D.C. that evening.

Inaugural celebrations began on Sunday, January 18. Hundreds of thousands of people attended a mega-concert titled the "We Are One" inaugural celebration. The performers represented a wide array of music. There was opera singer Renee Fleming; rockers U2 and Bruce Springsteen; R&B singers Stevie Wonder and Beyonce; jazz pianist Herbie Hancock; hip hop performer will.i.am; and country star Garth Brooks, a registered Republican.[25] Interspersed with the musical renderings were readings by celebrities of all races and religions such as Queen Latifah, Jack Black, Tom Hanks, Rosario Dawson, Tiger Woods, Steve Carell, and Ashley Judd.

The next day was Martin Luther King Day. It has become a tradition for people to volunteer to help others on the holiday. Obama spent his last day as president-elect painting the inside of a home for troubled teens in Washington, D.C. Although it was a serious project,

Obama showed his sense of humor. He said as he was painting, "This is good practice 'cause I'm moving to a new house tomorrow."[26] He joked about his lack of ability with electrical work and said he chose to paint because, "It's not rocket science. You take the pole and the roller, then you roll. But you do need to apply some elbow grease—like everything else we do."[27] Obama was one of about one million people across the country who volunteered their time that day to help less fortunate people.[28]

There was a huge rush of anticipation for Obama to finally take the oath of office at noon on January 20. About a million and a half people gathered on the National Mall to witness the historic event.[29] Just before noon, reverends Rick Warren and Joseph Lowery, an eighty-seven-year old veteran of the civil rights movement, offered prayers. Music legend Aretha Franklin then sang, "My Country 'Tis of Thee."

A little after noon, Obama was sworn in as president of the United States. He then gave a fairly short inaugural speech,

President-Elect Obama helps paint one of the walls of Sasha Bruce House, a teen shelter in Washington, D.C., on Martin Luther King Day, January 19, 2009.

just eighteen minutes long. He discussed the problems facing the United States and how hard work and self-sacrifice can repair them. He pronounced:

> In reaffirming the greatness of our nation, we understand that greatness is never a given. It must be earned. Our journey has never been one of shortcuts or settling for less. It has not been the path for the fainthearted—for those who prefer leisure over work, or seek only the pleasures of riches and fame. Rather, it has been the risk-takers, the doers, the makers of things—some celebrated, but more often men and women obscure in their labor—who have carried us up the long, rugged path toward prosperity and freedom.
>
> This is the journey we continue today. We remain the most prosperous, powerful nation on Earth. Our workers are no less productive than when this crisis began. Our minds are no less inventive, our goods and services no less needed than they were last week or last month or last year. Our capacity remains undiminished. But our time of standing pat, of protecting narrow interests and putting off unpleasant decisions—that time has surely passed. Starting today, we must pick ourselves up, dust ourselves off, and begin again the work of remaking America.[30]

He also appealed to Muslim nations in his speech. He offered to meet them halfway if they reject tyranny and terrorism. Many saw it as an outright rejection of Bush's hard line stands against the Muslim world. Obama stated:

Barack Obama takes the oath of office as he is sworn in as the 44th president of the United States on January 20, 2009.

To the Muslim world, we seek a new way forward, based on mutual interest and mutual respect. To those leaders around the globe who seek to sow conflict, or blame their society's ills on the West: Know that your people will judge you on what you can build, not what you destroy. To those who cling to power through corruption and deceit and the silencing of dissent, know that you are on the wrong side of history; but that we will extend a hand if you are willing to unclench your fist.[31]

Obama stressed that Americans can meet the tough challenges ahead. He called for cooperation.

Today I say to you that the challenges we face are real. They are serious and they are many. They will not be met easily or in a short span of time. But know this, America: They will be met.

On this day, we gather because we have chosen hope over fear, unity of purpose over conflict and discord.[32]

After his speech, Obama and his family participated in the traditional inaugural parade march through

President Obama and First Lady Michelle Obama dance together during the Commander in Chief Inaugural Ball at the National Building Museum in Washington, D.C.

downtown Washington. When the parade concluded, they went to the White house to change into their formal clothes. That night they made appearances at ten inaugural balls. While most were traditional formal balls, Obama planned a different type of ball—a youth ball. It was meant for people between the ages of eighteen and thirty-five. However, most who attended were no older than twenty-five. The Youth Ball featured performers such as Kid Rock, Kanye West, and Fall Out Boy. Obama had planned it to show appreciation for so many young people who played a very important role helping Obama get elected.

After the balls were over in the early morning hours of January 21, the Obamas went back to the White House for a good night's sleep. When daylight came, Barack Obama began his first day's work as president of the United States.

Obama's story—his journey as son of an African immigrant in Hawaii to the White House—and what it said about the United States was summed up by rap artist and mogul Sean "P. Diddy" Combs. The evening before the inauguration, Combs marveled, "It's such a proud moment. I'm so happy that the world gets to see that this is truly what America is, what America's about."[33]

Chronology

1961—Born on August 4 in Honolulu, Hawaii.

1963—Father leaves home.

1967—Moves with family to Indonesia.

1971—Moves with family back to Hawaii; begins attending Punahou School; father returns from Africa for visit.

1979—Graduates from Punahou School; begins studies at Occidental College in Los Angeles.

1981—Transfers to Columbia University in New York City.

1983—Graduates from Columbia University; takes job with Business International Corporation in New York City.

1984—Moves to Chicago to work as community organizer.

1987—Makes emotional trip to visit family in Kenya.

1988—Begins Harvard University Law School.

1989—Works as summer intern at law firm in Chicago where he meets Michelle Robinson.

1990–1991—President of Harvard Law Review.

1991—Graduates from Harvard University Law School; takes job with law firm of Miner, Barnhill & Galland in Chicago.

1992—Executive director of Illinois Project Vote; marries Michelle Robinson; begins teaching at University of Chicago Law School.

1995—Memoir, *Dreams From My Father*, is published.

1997–2004—Serves as Illinois State senator.

1999—Daughter Malia is born.

2000—Loses primary election in race for Democratic party nominee for United States House of Representatives.

2001—Daughter Sasha is born.

2004—Delivers keynote address at Democratic National Convention in Boston.

2005—Begins serving as United States senator from Illinois.

2006—Book, *The Audacity of Hope*, is published.

2007—Announces candidacy for Democratic party nomination for president of the United States in Springfield, Illinois, on February 10, 2007.

2008—*November 4:* Is elected 44th president of the United States.

2009—*January 20:* Presidential Inauguration of Barack Obama.

Chapter Notes

Chapter 1. On Stage in Front of the World

1. Todd Leopold, transcript of "The Democrats' calm rock star," *Cable News Network*, August 6, 2004, <http://www.cnn.com/2004/ALLPOLITICS/07/27/barack.obama/index.html> (February 25, 2007).

2. Personal appearance by Barack Obama at Keene State College, Keene, New Hampshire, April 2, 2007.

3. Leopold.

4. "Obama: Time to reclaim America's promise," *Cable News Network*, July 28, 2004, <http://www.cnn.com/2004/ALLPOLITICS/07/27/dems.obama.transcript/index.html> (February 25, 2007).

5. Tina Brown, "Barack Obama, Shaking Up The Sound-Bite Culture," EBSCOhost, (January 23, 2007), originally appeared in *The Washington Post*, August 5, 2004.

6. "Pundits Scorecard," *Cable News Network*, July 28, 2004, <http://www.cnn.com/ELECTION/2004/special/president/convention/dnc/press.pundits/archive/index.072804.html> (February 25, 2007).

7. Ibid.

Chapter 2. Life With Tutu and Lolo

1. Barack Obama, *Dreams from My Father* (New York: Three Rivers Press, 2004), p. 12.

2. Barack Obama, *The Audacity of Hope* (New York: Crown Publishers, 2006), p. 204.

3. Ibid. p. 203.

4. Julia Suryakusuma, "Obama for President . . . of Indonesia," *The Jakarta Post*, November 29, 2006, <http://www.thejakartapost.com/yesterdaydetail.asp?fileid=20061129.F03> (March 16, 2007).

5. Obama, *Dreams from My Father*, p. 30.

6. Ibid., pp. 51–52.

Chapter 3. Days at Punahou

1. Barack Obama, *Dreams from My Father* (New York: Three Rivers Press, 2004), p. 58.

2. Personal interview with Bernice Bowers, May 6, 2007.

3. Ibid.

4. Obama, p. 60.

5. Steve Dougherty, *Hopes and Dreams: The Story of Barack Obama* (New York: Black Dog & Leventhal Publishers, 2007), p. 46.

6. B. J. Reyes, "Punahou left lasting impression on Obama," *Honolulu Star-Bulletin*, February 8, 2007, <http://starbulletin.com/ 2007/02/08/news/story02.html> (March 16, 2007).

7. Personal interview with Bernice Bowers.

8. Obama, p. 86.

9. Reyes.

10. Personal e-mail from Bernice Bowers, originally ran in *Ka Wai Ola*, May 1979, 26th ed., Honolulu, Hawaii: Punahou School.

11. Personal interview with Bernice Bowers.

12. Ibid.

13. *60 Minutes*, CBS Broadcasting, Inc., Tom Anderson and L. Franklin Devine producers, February 11, 2007.

14. Obama, p. 97.

Chapter 4. "Not as Long as You Say It Right"

1. Larry Gordon, "Occidental recalls 'Barry' Obama," *Los Angeles Times*, January 29, 2007. <http://www.latimes.com/news/ local/la-me-oxy29jan29,0,2099497,full.story?coll=la-home-local> (March 16, 2007).

2. Personal interview with Eric Newhall, May 2, 2007.

3. Ibid.

4. *60 Minutes*, CBS Broadcasting, Inc., Tom Anderson and L. Franklin Devine producers, February 11, 2007.

5. Barack Obama, *Dreams from My Father* (New York: Three Rivers Press, 2004), pp. 99–100.

6. Ibid., p. 102.

7. Ibid., p. 104.

8. Personal interview with Eric Newhall.

9. Gordon.

10. Shira Boss-Bicak, "Barack Obama '83: Is He the New Face of The Democratic Party?" *Columbia College Today*, January 2005, (March 16, 2007).

Chapter 5. The World of Business

1. Barack Obama, *Dreams from My Father*, (New York: Three Rivers Press, 2004), p. 135.

2. Personal appearance by Barack Obama at Keene State College, Keene, New Hampshire, April 2, 2007.

3. Steve Dougherty, *Hopes and Dreams: The Story of Barack Obama* (New York: Black Dog & Leventhal Publishers, 2007), p. 63.

4. Peter Slevin, "For Clinton and Obama, a Common Ideological Touchstone," *The Washington Post*, March 25, 2007, <http://www.washingtonpost.com/wp-dyn/content/article/2007/03/24/AR2007032401152_pf.html> (March 29, 2007).

Chapter 6. The Organizer

1. Peter Slevin, "For Clinton and Obama, a Common Ideological Touchstone," *The Washington Post*, March 25, 2007, <http://www.washingtonpost.com/wp-dyn/content/article/2007/03/24/AR2007032401152_pf.html> (March 29, 2007).

2. Barack Obama, *Dreams from My Father* (New York: Three Rivers Press, 2004), p. 215.

3. Ibid., pp. 220–221.

4. Personal appearance by Barack Obama at Keene State College, Keene, New Hampshire, April 2, 2007.

5. Transcript of Tavis Smiley television program, October 23, 2006, <http://www.pbs.org/kcet/tavissmiley/archive/200610/20061023_obama.html> (March 19, 2007).

6. Ibid.

Chapter 7. His Father's Past and His Own Future

1. Barack Obama, *Dreams from My Father* (New York: Three Rivers Press, 2004), p. 399.

2. Ibid., p. 437.

3. William Finnegan, "The Candidate," *The New Yorker*, May 31, 2004, <http://www.newyorker.com/archive/2004/05/31/040531fa_fact1> (March 16, 2007).

4. Personal interview with Bradford Berenson, May 8, 2007.

5. Ibid.

6. Ibid.

7. Ibid.

8. Carol Platt Liebau, "The Barack I Knew," *www.Townhall.com*, March 5, 2005, <http://www.townhall.com/columnists/CarolPlattLiebau/2007/03/05/the_barack_i_knew> (April 4, 2007).

9. Jodi Kantor, "In Law School, Obama Found Political Voice," *The New York Times*, January 28, 2007,

<http://www.nytimes.com/2007/01/28/us/politics/28obama.html?ex=1175832000&en=f6443e4d5a93bfe1&ei=5070> (April 4, 2007).

10. Jonathan Alter, "The Audacity of Hope," *Newsweek*, December 27, 2004–January 3, 2005, pp. 82–83.

11. Personal interview with Judson H. Miner, May 4, 2007.

12. Transcript of "Rising Star," *News Hour with Jim Lehrer*, July 27, 2004, <http://www.pbs.org/newshour/bb/politics/july-dec04/obama_7-27.html> (April 25, 2007).

13. Personal interview with Judson H. Miner.

14. Finnegan.

15. Obama, p. 442.

16. "Obama delivers keynote address at Celebration of Black Alumni," *Harvard University*, September 16, 2005, <http://www.law.harvard.edu/news/2005/09/16_obama.php> (April 4, 2007).

Chapter 8. In the Footsteps of Lincoln

1. Noam Scheiber, "Race Against History," EBSCOhost, *New Republic*, March 31, 2004, (January 23, 2007).

2. Barack Obama, *The Audacity of Hope* (New York: Crown Publishers, 2006), p. 1.

3. William Finnegan, "The Candidate," *The New Yorker*, May 31, 2004, <http://www.newyorker.com/archive/2004/05/31/040531fa_fact1> (March 16, 2007).

4. Judy Keen, "The big question about Barack Obama," EBSCOhost, *USA Today*, January 17, 2007, <http://www.usatoday.com/news/washington/2007-01-16-obama-experience-cover_x.htm> (January 23, 2007).

5. Obama, *The Audacity of Hope*, p. 59.

6. Shira Boss-Bicak, "Barack Obama '83: Is He the New Face of The Democratic Party?" *Columbia College Today*, January 2005, <http://www.college.columbia.edu/cct/jan05/cover.php> (March 16, 2007).

7. Obama, *The Audacity of Hope*, p. 105.

8. Scheiber.

9. Boss-Bicak.

10. Obama, *The Audacity of Hope*, p. 106.

11. Scheiber.

12. Obama, *The Audacity of Hope*, p. 107.

13. "Remarks of Illinois State Sen. Barack Obama Against Going to War with Iraq," *Barack Obama official Web site*, October 2,

CHAPTER NOTES

2002, <http://www.barackobama.com/2002/10/02/remarks_of_
illinois_state_sen.php> (April 19, 2007).

14. Ibid.

Chapter 9. "Are You Making Other People's Lives a Little Bit Better?"

1. William Finnegan, "The Candidate," *The New Yorker*, May 31,
2004, <http://www.newyorker.com/archive/2004/05/31/040531fa_
fact1> (March 16, 2007).

2. Ibid.

3. Ibid.

4. Noam Scheiber, "Race Against History," EBSCOhost, *New
Republic*, March 31, 2004, <http://www.cbsnews.com/stories/2004/
09/08/politics/main641858.shtml> (January 23, 2007).

5. Steve Dougherty, *Hopes and Dreams: The Story of Barack
Obama* (New York: Black Dog & Leventhal Publishers, 2007), p. 89.

6. Associated Press, "Here's What Jesus Wouldn't Do," *CBS
News*, September 8, 2004, <http://www.cbsnews.com/stories/2004/
09/08/politics/main641858.shtml> (April 23, 2007).

7. Election results US Senate/Illinois, *CNN*, <http://www.cnn.
com/ELECTION/2004/pages/results/states/IL/S/01/index.html>
(April 23, 2007).

8. Ben Wallace-Wells, "Destiny's Child," *Rolling Stone*,
February 22, 2007, p. 49.

9. Ibid.

10. Chuck Goudie, "Obama meets with Arafat's successor,"
WLS-TV, January 12, 2006, <http://abclocal.go.com/wls/story?
section=local&id=3806933> (April 24, 2007).

11. "Screaming crowds welcome U.S. senator 'home,'" *CNN*,
August 27, 2006, <http://edition.cnn.com/2006/WORLD/africa/08/
26/kenya.obama/index.html> (April 24, 2007).

12. Ibid.

13. Ibid.

14. "President Bush Signs Coburn-Obama Transparency Act,"
Tom Coburn U.S. Senate Office, September 26, 2006, <http://coburn.
senate.gov/ffm/index.cfm?FuseAction=LegislativeFloorAction.
Home&ContentRecord_id=eb582f19-802a-23ad-41db-7a7cb464cfdb>
(April 24, 2007).

15. Krystin E. Kasak, "Obama introduces measure to bring
troops home: Act calls for government in Iraq to be accountable,"
(Northwest Indiana) *The Times*, appeared February 7, 2007,

<http://nwitimes.com/articles/2007/02/07/news/illiana/
doc65cc98d8dc6506b28625727b0011edb5.txt> (April 24, 2007).

16. Transcript of "Keeping Hope Alive," *The Oprah Winfrey Show*, October 18, 2006, <http://www2.oprah.com/tows/slide/
200610/20061018/slide_20061018_284_112.jhtml> (April 5, 2007).

17. Christi Parsons, "Obama: I'm running for president," *Chicago Tribune*, February 10, 2007, <http://www.chicagotribune.
com/news/local/chi-070210obama-parsons1-story,1,6611405.story?
coll=chi&ctrack=1&cset=true> (February 10, 2007).

18. "Full Text of Senator Barack Obama's Announcement for President," *Obama '08*, February 10, 2007, <http://www.barackobama.
com/2007/02/10/remarks_of_senator_barack_obam_11.php>
(April 24, 2007).

19. Judy Keen, "The big question about Barack Obama," EBSCOhost, *USA Today*, January 17, 2007, <http://www.usatoday.
com/news/washington/2007-01-16-obama-experience-cover_x.htm>
(January 23, 2007).

20. Jonathan Alter, "Is America Ready," *Newsweek*, December 25, 2006–January 1, 2007, p. 38.

21. *The Colbert Report*, Comedy Partners, broadcast February 20, 2007.

22. *60 Minutes*, CBS Broadcasting, Inc., Tom Anderson and L. Franklin Devine producers, broadcast February 11, 2007.

23. David Bauder, "Story about Obama's youthful schooling offers lessons as long campaign starts," Associated Press, *Keene Sentinel* (N.H.), TV Week section, p. 9.

24. "Obama warns Pakistan on al-Qaeda," *BBC News*, August 1, 2007, <http://news.bbc.co.uk/2/hi/americas/6926663.stm>
(September 9, 2007).

25. "Keeping Hope Alive," *The Oprah Winfrey Show*.

Chapter 10. Change Comes to America

1. Dan Balz, "Candidates Unite in Criticizing Bush," *The Washington Post*, April 27, 2007, <http://www.washingtonpost.com/
wp-dyn/content/article/2007/04/26/AR2007042602593.html>
(December 16, 2008).

2. "Results: Iowa," *CNN.com*, August 20, 2008, <http://www.
cnn.com/ELECTION/2008/primaries/results/state/#IA>
(December 16, 2008).

3. "Clinton, McCain Bids Energized in New Hampshire," *CNN.com*, January 9, 2008, <http://www.cnn.com/2008/

POLITICS/01/09/primary.main/index.html?iref=newssearch>
(December 16, 2008).

    4. "Results: New Hampshire," *CNN.com*, August 20, 2008,
<http://www.cnn.com/ELECTION/2008/primaries/results/state/
#NH> (December 16, 2008).

    5. Brian Ross and Rehab El-Buri, "Obama's Pastor: God Damn
America, U.S. to Blame for 9/11," *ABC News*, <http://abcnews.
go.com/Blotter/story?id=4443788> (December 22, 2008).

    6. "The Long Siege," *Newsweek*, November 17, 2008, p. 67.

    7. "Remarks by Barack Obama: 'A More Perfect Union,'" *The
Christian Science Monitor*, March 19, 2008, <http://www.csmonitor.
com/2008/0319/p25s01-uspo.html> (December 23, 2008).

    8. Ibid.

    9. Ibid.

    10. "The Long Siege," p. 71.

    11. Joe Klein, "Ready to Lead," originally appeared in *Time*,
November 3, 2008; reproduced in *President Obama: The Path To the
White House*, Richard Stengel, ed. (New York: Time Books, 2008),
p. 88.

    12. "Transcript," *Bill Moyers Journal*, April 25, 2008, <http://
www.pbs.org/moyers/journal/04252008/transcript1.html> (January 21,
2009).

    13. Jeff Zeleny, "Obama Says He's Outraged by Ex-Pastor's
Comments," *The New York Times*, April 29, 2008, <http://thecaucus.
blogs.nytimes.com/2008/04/29/obama-says-hes-outraged-by-ex-
pastors-comments/?hp> (January 21, 2009).

    14. Andrew Krukowski, "Record 38 Million Watched Obama
Speech on 10 Networks," *TV Week*, August 29, 2008, <http://www.
tvweek.com/news/2008/08/record_38_million_watched_obam.php>
(December 23, 2008).

    15. "Barack Obama's Acceptance Speech," *The New York Times*,
August 28, 2008, <http://elections.nytimes.com/2008/president/
conventions/videos/transcripts/20080828_OBAMA_SPEECH.html>
(December 24, 2008).

    16. Ibid.

    17. Scott Shane, "Obama and '60s Bomber: A Look Into
Crossed Paths," *The New York Times*, October 3, 2008, <http://www.
nytimes.com/glogin?URI=http://www.nytimes.com/2008/10/04/us/
politics/04ayers.html&OQ=_rQ3D2&OP=681983b8Q2FQ5Dq5T
Q5Dm!IQ2A0!!2iQ5DipplQ5D(pQ5DpQ20Q5DkQ2AQ5Dr!yN2
NIQ2AQ5DpQ20CO50Q2AA42)y> (December 24, 2008).

18. Ibid.

19. "Palin Hits Obama for 'Terrorist' Connection," *CNN.com*, October 5, 2008, <http://m.cnn.com/cnn/lt_ne/lt_ne/detail/178228> (December 24, 2008).

20. "The Third McCain-Obama Presidential Debate," *Commission on Presidential Debates*, October 15, 2008, <http://www.debates.org/pages/trans2008d.html> (December 24, 2008).

21. Shailagh Murray, "Obama's Grandmother Dies," *The Washington Post*, November 3, 2008, <http://voices.washingtonpost.com/the-trail/2008/11/03/obamas_grandmother_dies.html> (January 20, 2009).

22. "Obama's Grandmother Dies After Battle with Cancer," *CNN.com*, November 3, 2008, <http://www.cnn.com/2008/POLITICS/11/03/obama.grandma/index.html> (January 20, 2009).

23. "2008 Election Coverage," *USA Today*, <http://www.usatoday.com/news/politics/default.htm> (December 28, 2008)

24. Ibid.

25. "In His Own Words: Excerpts From Victory Speech: Chicago, Nov. 4, 2008," *Newsweek Special Commemorative Issue: Obama's American Dream*, November 2008, p. 80.

26. Jann S. Wenner, "How Obama Won," *Rolling Stone*, November 27, 2008, p. 52.

Chapter 11. "The Journey We Continue Today"

1. *The Star-Ledger* (Newark, N.J.) front page, November 5, 2008, <http://www.newseum.org> (November 16, 2008).

2. *USA Today* front page, November 6, 2008.

3. Rick Hampson, "For Many, a Sense That a New Era Is Here," *USA Today*, November 6, 2008, p. 1A.

4. *The Anniston Star* front page, November 5, 2008, <http://www.newseum.org> (November 16, 2008).

5. *The Times of London* front page, November 5, 2008, <http://www.timesonline.co.uk> (November 5, 2008).

6. Hampson.

7. Joe Klein, "Obama's Team of Rivals," *Time*, June 18, 2008, <http://www.time.com/time/politics/article/0,8599,1815849,00.html> (January 17, 2009).

8. Associated Press, "Official: Gates to Stay at Pentagon," *The Chicago Sun-Times*, November 25, 2008,

CHAPTER NOTES

<http://www.suntimes.com/news/politics/obama/1299669,gates-defense-stay112508.article> (January 8, 2009).

9. Ibid.

10. *A Barbara Walters Special*, ABC News, broadcast November 26, 2008.

11. "Barack Obama: We Want a Shelter Dog . . . a Mutt Like Me!" *Usmagazine.com*, November 7, 2008, <http://www.usmagazine.com/news/barack-obama-we-want-a-shelter-dog-a-mutt-like-me> (January 21, 2009).

12. *A Barbara Walters Special*.

13. "Bill Richardson Bows Out of Commerce Secretary Job," *CNN.com*, January 5, 2009, <http://www.cnn.com/2009/POLITICS/01/04/richardson.withdrawal/index.html> (January 8, 2009).

14. David Jackson and Mimi Hall, "Obama Hails 'Extraordinary' Power Lunch," *USA Today*, January 8, 2009, p. 5A.

15. Ben Feller, "Five Living Presidents Hold Meeting," *The Keene Sentinel*, January 8, 2009, p. 15.

16. Ibid.

17. Jennifer Loven, "Obama Pitches Economic Plan," *The Keene Sentinel*, January 8, 2009, p. 5.

18. Chris Cillizza, "Obama Bets Big on Big Government," *The Washington Post*, January 8, 2009, <http://voices.washingtonpost.com/thefix/2009/01/obama_bets_big_on_big_governme.html> (January 8, 2009).

19. "Speech Excerpts Released," *The Washington Post*, January 8, 2009, <http://voices.washingtonpost.com/thefix/2009/01/obama_bets_big_on_big_governme.html> (January 8, 2009).

20. David Colton, "Obama, Spider-Man on the Same Page," *USA Today*, January 8, 2009, p. 1D.

21. "New York City Trio Accused of Beating up Blacks After Barack Obama's Election Victory," *The Chicago Sun-Times*, January 8, 2009, <http://www.suntimes.com/news/nation/1368479,w-barack-obama-racism-attacks010809.article> (January 8, 2008).

22. *A Barbara Walters Special*.

23. Barack Obama, "What I Want for You—and Every Child in America," *Parade*, January 18, 2009, pp. 4–5.

24. Kathleen Gray and Todd Spangler, "Train Takes Obama on Momentous D.C. Trip," *Detroit Free Press*, January 18, 2009, <http://www.freep.com/article/20090118/OBAMAINAUGURATION10/901180462/1285/NEWS15/Train+takes+Obama+on+momentous+D.C.+trip> (January 19, 2009).

25. Maria Puente and Elysa Gardner, "The Art of the Possible," *USA Today*, January 19, 2009, p. D1.

26. Maggie Haberman, "Hey, When You're Done With That, Can You Fix the Economy?" *New York Post*, January 20, 2009, p. 5.

27. Ibid.

28. Andrea Stone, "Turnout Great to Honor MLK With Service," *USA Today*, January 20, 2009, p. 6A.

29. "U.S. Celebrates as President Obama Vows New Era," *CNN.com*, January 20, 2009, <http://www.cnn.com/2009/POLITICS/01/20/obama.inauguration/index.html> (January 20, 2009).

30. "Obama's Inaugural Speech," *CNN.com*, January 20, 2009, <http://www.cnn.com/2009/POLITICS/01/20/obama.politics/index.html?iref=mpstoryview> (January 20, 2009).

31. Ibid.

32. Ibid.

33. *Larry King Live*, CNN, broadcast January 19, 2009.

Further Reading

Books

Devaney, Sherri and Mark Devaney. *Barack Obama*. Detroit: Lucent Books, 2007.

Dougherty, Steve. *Hopes and Dreams: The Story of Barack Obama*. New York: Black Dog & Leventhal Publishers, 2007.

Obama, Barack. *The Audacity of Hope: Thoughts on Reclaiming the American Dream*. New York: Crown Publishers, 2006.

Obama, Barack. *Dreams From My Father: A Story of Race and Inheritance*. New York: Times Books, 2005.

Internet Addresses

President Barack Obama
<http://whitehouse.gov/administration/president_obama/>

Barack Obama Featured Biography
<http://www.biography.com/featured-biography/barack-obama/index.jsp>

Index

Page numbers for photographs are in **boldface** type.

INDEX